THE
SCOUT'S
DUTCH OVEN COOKBOOK

TIM AND CHRISTINE CONNERS

FALCONGUIDES

GUILFORD, CONNECTICUT
HELENA, MONTANA

AN IMPRINT OF GLOBE PEQUOT PRESS

To buy books in quantity for corporate use
or incentives, call **(800) 962–0973**
or e-mail **premiums@GlobePequot.com**.

FALCONGUIDES®

FalconGuides is an imprint of Globe Pequot Press.

Falcon, FalconGuides, and Outfit Your Mind are registered trademarks of
Morris Book Publishing, LLC.

Text design: Sheryl P. Kober
Project editor: Julie Marsh
Layout: Mary Ballachino

Library of Congress Cataloging-in-Publication Data is available on file.

ISBN 978-0-7627-7808-9

Printed in the United States of America

10 9 8 7 6 5 4 3 2 1

MIX
Paper from
responsible sources
FSC® C005010

CONTENTS

DEDICATION

To the countless leaders throughout Boy Scouts of America whose concern and self-sacrifice have helped successfully guide millions of our boys through the trials of youth into manhood.

BENEDICTION

He has shown kindness by giving you rain from heaven and crops in their seasons; he provides you with plenty of food and fills your hearts with joy.
—Acts 14:17 (NIV)

ACKNOWLEDGMENTS

To the dozens of Scout leaders from across the country who answered our call for recipes, tips, and suggestions, you have our heartfelt gratitude. Without your Dutch-oven genius, this book would not have been possible. We'd like to especially recognize the talents and contributions of longtime camp chef Delano LaGow of Three Fires Council's Troop 31.

Scott Daniels, now the former managing editor for *Scouting* magazine, cleared the path once again. Max Phelps, director of outdoor sales at Globe Pequot Press, sold the idea. And Jessica Haberman, acquisitions editor at Globe, made it real. Especially to you three, thank you!

To Marlynn Griffin, Ken Harbison, Melissa Moore, and Linda Tinker, all of whom assisted with testing, and to Jenny Lamb (www.frontierfreedom.com) and John Malachowski for their photography, you have our sincere appreciation. And to Scott Simerly and Troop 204 for freely sharing hundreds of their wonderful photographs, a very hearty thanks.

Introduction

Most people outside the world of Boy Scouts don't have a clue what a camp Dutch oven is. Don't believe it? Try this on your non-Scouting friends: Ask them to describe a "camp Dutch oven." Prepare to enjoy the blank stares and ridiculous answers you receive in return.

Of course, the opposite is true for those of us in Scouting. We learn early about the wonders of this incredible cooking instrument. The Dutch oven is as much a part of the Boy Scouts as the neckerchief and the Pinewood Derby. Just try to count all the ovens you see at the next Camporee. They are found *everywhere* Scouts go to camp.

The Dutch oven is so popular in Scouting because it is easy to use, it produces outstanding results, and it is very versatile. Only a lousy recipe or gross negligence can threaten a dish from a Dutch oven. Even then, the results are often surprisingly good.

Dutch ovens are impressively massive compared to standard cookware. They come in many sizes. The largest ovens can feed dozens of people. Most are made from heavy cast iron. This bulk is what makes the Dutch oven a great cooking device. Thick walls distribute heat from all directions, evenly warming food while reducing the chance of burning. The heavy lid traps moisture, preventing food from drying out while cooking. The cast iron retains heat long after the oven is taken from the coals or fire, keeping food warm throughout mealtime, even in cold weather.

Dutch ovens are extremely durable, so they are well suited to the rough world of outdoor camp life. Properly seasoned cast-iron ovens are easy to clean because of their natural nonstick coating. And Dutch ovens can cook almost anything. They can be used to fry, sauté, bake, stew, roast, and slow-cook—any time of day, nearly any type of meal.

The Dutch oven's design has been in use for at least three hundred years. The best ovens originally came from the Netherlands, thus the name. But it wasn't long before Britain became a leading manufacturer of cast-iron cookware. Many Dutch ovens were exported to the growing colony in America, where they became very popular.

Lewis and Clark's Dutch oven was one of their most valued possessions during their expedition across the American frontier. In fact, it was in early America that the practical "camp" Dutch oven design, sporting short legs and a flanged lid, came into common use. It is this very same design that we continue to use in camp today.

With camp cookery as popular as ever within Scouting, this book continues the tradition founded in our pioneering past by focusing solely on the art of camp Dutch oven cooking. This is an all-in-one manual for Boy Scouts and their leaders, containing enough information to support a mastery of basic concepts for those new to Dutch oven cooking, while providing many challenges for advanced outdoor chefs.

The camp Dutch oven at work. SCOTT H. SIMERLY SR.

The introductory information and appendices in this book contain reference material that cooks of any skill level should find useful. But cooking with a Dutch oven is straightforward, with less of an emphasis on technique compared to other cooking methods. The recipes are in the spotlight here, and they form the backbone of the book. These are the true test of the camp chef's skills and produce a reward for effort to be appreciated by many.

Over one hundred outstanding recipes are included, covering a wide range of cooking styles and techniques and spanning all meal categories. Every recipe was provided by a leader from within Boy Scouts, each recipe having been carefully selected from a much larger initial collection. All were thoroughly tested to ensure success in camp.

As long as the outdoors continues to draw people to it, and for as long as Scouts continue to gather together with only the sky above, camp cookery will remain an essential part of Scoutcraft. And in this setting, the Dutch oven is certain to endure as the centerpiece of camp cooking.

USING THIS BOOK TO PLAN AND PREPARE YOUR MEALS

The following sections explain the general layout of this cookbook and how the information included can specifically assist with meal planning.

The recipes in this book are its foundation and have been arranged to maximize the efficiency of the meal-planning process. Information is plainly presented to allow the reader to quickly judge the merits of a particular recipe while preparing for a Scout camping trip. Each recipe is clearly and logically structured for foolproof preparation once in camp.

Recipe Categories

Categorizing recipes is not as easy as it might seem. There are as many ways to organize a cookbook as there are eating styles and preferences. The approach that appears to satisfy most people is to begin by organizing entrees according to the meal category where they best belong: breakfast, lunch, or dinner. Those recipes that cannot be tagged as a main dish are grouped into three other primary categories: side dishes, breads, and snacks and desserts.

The lunch category deserves special mention, as it is always tricky to decide which meals are suitable to call "lunch." This section was constructed around several premises, the most important being that the camp cook will usually seek easier meals so Scouts can rapidly move on to scheduled activities in the early afternoon. Therefore, the emphasis is on those recipes that can be quickly prepared, served, and recovered from. In fact, the embers from a leftover morning campfire are all that are needed to cook those recipes that can tolerate a non-exact coal count. Only those recipes with an estimated total preparation time of an hour or less were included in the lunch category. The cook desiring to prepare a more involved meal at midday might also consult the recipes in the dinner section, many of which perform equally well at the noon hour.

Servings

From eight to twelve servings can be expected from most of the recipes in this book, enough to feed a full Scout Patrol and a few senior Scouters. Some of the recipes serve as many as twenty people. Others are designed to feed groups as small as four to six. It's a straightforward task to multiply recipes as required to meet the needs of a larger group size, especially when using Dutch ovens. But it's often less easy to scale down a dish, which is why an assortment of recipes are included for the smaller groups.

For consistency, serving estimates assume the target audience to be active teenagers on a moderate caloric intake. Serving sizes were adjusted upward as credit for healthier recipes and downward for those with less desirable nutrition characteristics. Adjust your estimates according to your specific situation and preference.

The camp Dutch oven is an exceptionally versatile cooking instrument. CHRISTINE CONNERS

Challenge Level

A three-tier ranking was used to assign a cooking challenge level to each recipe: "easy," "moderate," or "difficult." The decision was based on the preparation and cleanup effort required, the sensitivity of the cooking technique to variation, and the attention to care necessary to avoid injury. Most of the recipes in this book have been tagged as "easy."

To avoid frustrating Scouts with an excessive number of difficult recipes, they are purposely few in number. But those that remain are valuable for two reasons: First, they are superb dishes worthy of the attempt; second, they are meant to serve as exercises for Scouts and leaders to further hone their skills and creativity. These recipes are intended to inspire you to reach for the next level and challenge yourselves.

Preparation Time

Total preparation time under pleasant weather conditions has been estimated for each recipe. Rounded to the nearest quarter-hour, this value includes the time required to prepare the coals through to serving the dish. It is assumed that the cook will flow the preparation steps in parallel whenever possible. For instance, while the coals are starting, other preparation steps can often be accomplished simultaneously. The recipes are written to best take advantage of this.

Preparation Instructions

Instructions for each recipe include a list of ingredients along with step-by-step directions, each logically grouped and presented in numerical sequence. The use of numerical sequencing in the preparation steps is intended to help the chef stay focused and to assist in the assignment of specific tasks for the Scouts. The majority of recipes are prepared completely in camp, but some require at-home preparation steps. Those that do clearly indicate so. Ingredient lists have been carefully selected to create less waste of key items.

Heating instructions are clear and consistent and provide high probability of success under a wide range of cooking conditions. To avoid confusion, an exact number of briquettes (coals) is specified for use on the lid and under the oven.

It's easy to control the heat in a camp Dutch oven using a coal-temperature conversion chart.

SCOTT H. SIMERLY SR.

Coal-Temperature Conversion Chart

Dutch Oven Diameter		Oven Temperature					
		325°F	350°F	375°F	400°F	425°F	450°F
8"	Total Briquettes	15	16	17	18	19	20
	On Lid	10	11	11	12	13	14
	Underneath Oven	5	5	6	6	6	6
10"	Total Briquettes	19	21	23	25	27	29
	On Lid	13	14	16	17	18	19
	Underneath Oven	6	7	7	8	9	10
12"	Total Briquettes	23	25	27	29	31	33
	On Lid	16	17	18	19	21	22
	Underneath Oven	7	8	9	10	10	11
14"	Total Briquettes	30	32	34	36	38	40
	On Lid	20	21	22	24	25	26
	Underneath Oven	10	11	12	12	13	14
16"	Total Briquettes	37	39	41	43	45	47
	On Lid	25	26	27	28	29	30
	Underneath Oven	12	13	14	15	16	17

If an actual baking temperature is required, say, to modify the recipe or to adapt it to a larger or smaller Dutch oven, the conversion chart above can be used to make the transformation by converting the specified coal count and Dutch oven size back into a temperature value. This conversion chart, based on data from Lodge Manufacturing, is very reliable when cooking with cast-iron stoves under pleasant weather using standard size, high-quality briquettes, fresh from the charcoal starter.

Options and Tips

Cooking options are provided for many of the recipes. Options differ from the main instructions and produce alternate endings to the recipe. Options included with a recipe are shown separately from the main preparation steps.

Likewise, contributors occasionally offered helpful tips that would assist the camp cook with purchasing ingredients or preparing the recipe in some way. As with options, tips not directly useful to the preparation steps are listed separately from the main body of the recipe. Recommendations and tips of a more generic nature, or applicable to a wider range of recipes and situations, are grouped separately in the following sections.

Required Equipment

A list of required cooking equipment follows each set of instructions, but not every item needed to prepare a recipe is listed. For example, a cooler or refrigeration device is obviously essential for keeping perishable foods safe. It is assumed that one is always available for use. Other items presumed to be basic equipment residing in any Scout cook's outdoor kitchen:

Food thermometer

Measuring cups and spoons

Can opener

Cutting and paring knives

Cutting board

Long-handle wooden spoons

Long-handle ladles

A food-grade greasing agent, such as vegetable oil

Serving plates, utensils, cups, and napkins

Wash basins, scrub pads, dish detergent, and towels

Hand sanitizer

Work table and serving table

It is also assumed the necessary tools and equipment will be available for preparing and managing the heat source required for the recipe, such as briquettes for the Dutch oven. These are discussed in a separate section.

Once a recipe's equipment needs go beyond the list of these basics, those requirements are listed with each recipe to head off any surprises in camp.

The real workhorses are the camp Dutch ovens. Four sizes are used to prepare all the recipes in this book: a 12-inch/6-quart oven, adequate for most of the recipes; a deep 14-inch/10-quart oven for roasting or baking tall items; a 16-inch/12-quart oven for large pizzas and the like; and a 10-inch/4-quart oven for smaller groups. Other sizes of Camp Dutch ovens are also available; while these can definitely be useful when adapting a dish for a different number of servings, they are not required to use this book.

When bowls, skillets, or cooking pots are specified for a recipe, "small," "medium," and "large" are used to approximate the capacity to do the job. Most troops already carry an assort-

A well-equipped camp kitchen. *SCOTT H. SIMERLY SR.*

ment of sizes for each of these cooking utensils. By having several sizes available at camp, you'll never find yourself in a pickle during food preparation. If ever in doubt on utensil size requirements, err on the side of larger capacity.

Contributor Information

Rounding out each recipe, you'll find information about the contributors. These are the field experts, the Scout leaders who made the book possible. You'll learn their names, scouting title, place of residence, and the troop or den and council they call home. Many contributors included anecdotes and stories to accompany their recipes. Useful and often humorous, anecdotes can be found at the top of each recipe.

Category System

When planning a menu for the outdoors, five key considerations are typically used when developing a list of candidate recipes: 1) the equipment available to the cook; 2) the number of people to prepare for; 3) the time that will be available to prepare the meal; 4) the level of skill or resources available to achieve good results; and 5) any special nutrition requirements.

Discussed earlier in this section, recipes are first grouped by meal category, forming the main recipe sections in the book. From there, the recipes have been sub-grouped by number of servings, estimated preparation time, and challenge level. These recipe characteristics are summarized in a red box in the sidebar of each recipe; the required Dutch oven size is included in the Required Equipment list for each recipe. This system specifically addresses the five key considerations discussed above.

Supplemental Information for the Camp Cook

Additional information is included in the front and back sections of the book to assist the outdoor chef. An important section on cooking safety highlights the most common risks found in the camp kitchen and what can be done to help reduce the probability of an accident. Be safe. Review this material, especially if you are new to camp cooking.

Along with safety comes skill, and an expert camp chef is far less likely to inflict injury or illness to either himself or to his fellow Scouts. A section on basic skills reviews the competencies that outdoor chefs should seek to understand and master, with an emphasis on cooking with Dutch ovens.

Most Dutch ovens are made from cast iron, and cast iron is tough stuff. But it is not impervious to improper care or abuse. There are several key points to keep in mind when using, cleaning, and storing cast iron cookware; this information is covered in a dedicated section. The section that immediately follows covers accessories essential for safe and enjoyable use of your Dutch oven.

For those who have never used a camp Dutch oven, a detailed tutorial rounds out the introduction of the book. This is a great launching point for the new Dutch oven chef. Based on an outstanding, easy-to-prepare recipe, *every* step of the process is detailed, from shopping for ingredients at the grocery store, through preparing the meal in camp, to cleaning up afterward.

The appendices cover a wide variety of helpful reference information, including kitchen measurement conversions, sources of camp cooking equipment, a bibliography of additional books and information on outdoor cooking, and techniques for reducing the environmental impact of camp cooking. Also included is a list of all Boy Scout merit badge requirements related to outdoor cooking that this cookbook can help Scouts to achieve.

Healthy Pairings

The Dutch oven is well known for creating some of the most wonderfully delicious and rich foods. But when cooking with a Dutch oven, wise choices and moderation are key to maintaining a reasonably healthy diet in camp.

When choosing recipes that lean toward higher fats and sugars, balance your meals with light salads or fresh vegetables. Pair a heavy entrée with a lighter after-dinner option, such as fresh fruit. If everyone's favorite decadent dessert is on the menu, choose a lighter dinner to go with it. Avoid serving multiple courses at a meal, which otherwise complicate meal planning and cleanup and also contribute to overeating.

Between meals, have healthy snacks available instead of fatty and sugary cookies and candy. Bananas, oranges, clementines, grapes, cherries, peaches, nectarines, plums, apples, and carrots are all easy to store and serve while in camp. In-shell peanuts and tortilla chips and salsa make for favorite between-meal snacks.

The evidence continues to mount that excessive soda consumption contributes to health complications. Drinks with electrolytes can be appropriate when the weather is warm; otherwise, make the mainstay cool water or juices with no added sugar, and only serve soda as an occasional treat.

Rich and decadent or lean and healthy, the Dutch oven can cook them all! SCOTT H. SIMERLY SR.

CAMP COOKING SAFETY

Paramount to all Scouting activities is the requirement that we conduct ourselves in a safe and responsible manner at all times and in all places. The camp kitchen presents some of the more significant hazards that a Scout will face during his stay outdoors, and yet the risks there are often taken for granted.

Most people have learned to successfully manage dangers in the home kitchen through caution and experience. But *camp* cooking presents many new and unique hazards that, if not appreciated and controlled, can cause severe injury or illness. The following information on cooking safety highlights the most common risks found in the camp kitchen and what can be done to help reduce the probability of an accident.

While the goal should always be zero accidents, minor injuries, including cuts and burns, are common in the camp kitchen. Keep the first-aid kit handy for these. But never acceptable are preventable serious injuries or food-borne illness. Extreme care and caution should *always* be used to prevent accidents that would otherwise send your Scouts or Scouters to the doctor or hospital.

Be careful. Searing hot metal can char your skin in an instant. Sharp knifes can go deep into your body before your brain has time to register what is happening. Heavy cast iron dropped on your foot can smash unprotected bones. Harmful bacteria left alive due to improper cooking can leave you dangerously ill.

Learn to respect *every* step of the cooking process. Always think about what you are about to do and ask yourself, "Is this safe?" If it isn't, or even if you are uncomfortable for reasons you don't understand, trust your instinct. Stop and determine how to do the job better, either by using more appropriate techniques and equipment or by asking others for assistance or advice.

And don't try to mimic the chefs you might see on TV. That fancy speed-chopping might look impressive, but it's dangerous if you don't know what you're doing. Slow down and move methodically. No matter how hungry the Scouts might be, no meal is worth compromising health and well-being.

With care and attention, any cooking risk can be managed to an acceptable level. The following list of guidelines for safety will help you do just that.

First aid in the field. *LICENSED BY SHUTTERSTOCK*

Supervision

- First and foremost, a responsible adult leader or mature Scout must always carefully supervise the cooking activities of less experienced Scouts, even more so when heat, sharp utensils, or raw meat are involved.

Food Poisoning

- Ensure that recipes containing raw meat or eggs are thoroughly cooked. Use a food thermometer to take several readings at various locations throughout the food being prepared. Minimum safe cooking temperatures vary by food type, but 165°F is high enough to kill all common food-borne pathogens. Use this value when in doubt.

- Cold and wet weather can significantly lower the temperature of the heat source and cookware. Prepare to increase the number of coals or the length of cooking time to compensate. Windy weather can have an unpredictable effect on cooking time, the temperature within the Dutch oven sometimes becoming uneven. The use of a food thermometer is especially recommended in all cases of adverse weather when cooking raw meat or eggs.

- Care should be taken when handling raw meat or eggs to prevent cross-contamination of other foods such as raw vegetables. When preparing raw meats, cutting surfaces and utensils should be dedicated *only* to this task or thoroughly washed with soap prior to use for other purposes. Avoid the common mistake of placing just-cooked food into an unwashed bowl or tray used earlier to mix or hold raw meats or eggs.

- Raw meat and eggs should be tightly sealed in a container or zip-lock bag and placed in a cooler until ready to use. To avoid cross-contamination, keep these items in their own cooler, separate from drinking ice, raw fruits, vegetables, cheese, beverages, or any other items that will not eventually be cooked at high temperature.

- Sanitize your work area with a good wipe-down both before and after the meal using antibacterial cleaners appropriate for the kitchen.

- Using soap and water or hand sanitizer, thoroughly clean your hands immediately after you've handled raw meat or eggs and before touching any other cooking instruments or ingredients. If you must repeatedly touch raw meat or eggs during preparation, then repeatedly sanitize your hands before handling anything else. Be compulsive about this. It's that important.

- All food that could potentially spoil, including leftovers, should be kept on ice in camp. To prolong the life of your ice, store coolers in a shady, cool, secure location, with lids tightly sealed. Covering the coolers with sleeping bags or blankets on a warm day will further insulate them.

- Be sure that any water used for cooking has been properly treated or purified before using. Do not simply assume that water from a camp spigot is safe to drink. Ask camp officials if you are unsure.

Cuts, Burns, and Broken Bones

- Use protective gear, such as leather barbecue gloves, on *both* hands when handling hot coals. Ensure that the gloves are long enough to protect your forearms. Closed-top shoes are also required. The top of your bare foot won't quickly forget a red-hot briquette landing snugly between your sandal straps.

- Cast-iron cookware is heavy. But a large Dutch oven filled to the brim with hot food is extremely heavy . . . and dangerous. Wear heat-proof gloves and closed-top footwear when handling hot and loaded cast iron. And if the oven is too heavy for you to safely handle alone, swallow your pride and ask someone for help.

- Cast iron retains heat for a long time after it is removed from the coals. This is a great quality for keeping food warm during meal time, but it also sets the stage for burn injuries to the unsuspecting. Before moving any cast iron with unprotected hands after the meal, carefully check to be sure the metal has cooled sufficiently. If it hasn't, or if you're unsure, use heat-proof gloves.

- Cutting utensils are inherently dangerous and should be handled with care. It may come as a surprise that dull cutting blades can be more dangerous than sharper instruments. Dull knife blades can slip much more easily when slicing or chopping and can quickly end up in the side of your finger instead of the food you're cutting. Keeping cutting blades sharp will help ensure they do what you expect them to do. When slicing and chopping, always keep your hands and fingers from under the blade or from in front of the knife tip.

- Extreme care should be taken when cleaning and storing sharp kitchen instruments. A knife at the bottom of a wash basin filled with soapy or dirty water is a potential booby trap for the unlucky dishwasher who doesn't know it's there. Don't leave knives hidden in soapy water. The same holds true when storing sharp utensils after cleaning. Knives, in particular, should be sheathed in a holder when placed back in storage.

Fire Safety

- All cooking must be performed in a fire-safe area of camp, clear of natural combustibles like dry leaves, grass, and trees and away from wooden structures. When cooking directly on the ground using coals, select a durable area covered in fireproof material such as rock, gravel, or bare earth. Be sure to follow any special open-fire restrictions established for your region. Ask camp officials about this when checking in. Always have a large bucket of water handy to douse any flames that may escape your fire-safe perimeter.

- Hot coals on the ground present a potential hazard during cooking but especially afterward. With the Dutch oven now off the heat, and with the coals likely ashed over, the threat lurking in your cooking area might go unnoticed. Notify your fellow Scouts of the danger of hot coals on the ground. Keep your cooking area safe and off-limits to all but essential personnel until the coals expire. Once the coals have fully cooled, discard the ash in a fire-safe manner appropriate for your camp.

- Unless vented, noxious fumes from burning coals will rise and concentrate at the apex of any roof under which cooking is performed. So when a kitchen tent or tarp structure is used for cooking in camp, the apex must be substantially higher than a tall person's head and with walls open and well ventilated on all sides. When cooking in a kitchen tent, be especially diligent to maintain a large fire-safe perimeter around the

Hot coals are an ever-present hazard to the careless and unwary. *TIM CONNERS*

coal tray. *Never attempt to cook in a sleeping tent, even a large one.* The fully enclosed walls will concentrate deadly gases and cause asphyxiation; or the tent floor or walls could rapidly catch fire and trap the occupants. A standard picnic canopy with low ceiling or partially enclosed side walls is also unsafe for cooking because the apex is at head height and the walls are often too low or poorly ventilated.

Allergies and Special Diets

- When planning a menu for an outing, ask your fellow Scouts and Scouters if any have food allergies or health issues that might require special dietary restrictions. Selecting recipes that meet everyone's needs might seem impossible in these circumstances, but many recipes can be modified to meet dietary requirements while satisfying everyone else in the group. This approach can be far easier on the cook than attempting to adhere to a parallel special-requirements menu.

Wild Animals

- Animals searching for food can pose a danger to the camp environment through aggression or disease. Unattended dirty dishes, unsecured garbage, and food items and coolers left in the open will all eventually attract unwanted animal attention. Wildlife that enjoys such goodies will surely come back for more, placing the animals at risk of harm along with the people who must interact with them or remove them. A neat and clean camp, with food and garbage properly and securely stored, is far less attractive to local fauna. Practice low-impact camping, and adhere to any food storage regulations unique to your area or camp.

No list can cover every danger lurking in any situation, and the above is surely no exception. But by learning to cook with a mind fixated on safety, you will be less likely to be caught by surprise or find yourself ill prepared.

BASIC SKILLS FOR THE DUTCH OVEN CHEF

The artisan is always learning. Skill-building spans a lifetime. And the challenge helps to keep a pastime exciting and enjoyable. But any activity quickly becomes frustrating without a strong foundation in the basic skills. So this section covers the essentials of outdoor cooking with Dutch ovens.

What Is a Camp Dutch Oven?

Before reviewing basic skills for the Dutch oven chef, it's helpful to know the differences in Dutch oven design, as there are two primary types: one for the *camp* and the other for the *kitchen*. While both are made from cast iron with heavy walls and come in a range of sizes, two prominent features distinguish the two types: First, the camp oven sports a trio of short legs instead of the completely smooth underside of the kitchen oven. Second, the camp oven has a flattened lid, flanged around the perimeter for holding coals, whereas the kitchen oven has a domed, flangeless lid that doesn't readily hold briquettes.

A kitchen Dutch oven, on the left, compared to a camp Dutch oven, on the upper right. *TIM CONNERS*

The reason for these differences is straightforward: The kitchen Dutch oven is designed to be used indoors on range burners and to rest on a wire rack in the kitchen oven, whereas the camp Dutch oven is designed to be used outdoors with briquettes placed under the oven and on the lid.

Selecting a Camp Dutch Oven

- When choosing a camp Dutch oven, look for one with walls of even thickness and free of pitting, a hefty bail wire handle, and a tight-fitting lid. A loop handle, located precisely in the center of the lid, is necessary on larger ovens for secure and balanced removal of a hot cover using a lid-lifter.

- A simple tab handle, instead of a loop handle, is used on the lids of some ovens, requiring pliers or vise-grips to remove. While acceptable on the smallest ovens, because of the compact size and lighter weight of the lid, this design is sometimes seen on larger ovens of poorer quality and should be avoided. Removing a large, heavy lid with pliers or grips is awkward and dangerous because the hot, coal-laden cover can easily slip from the tool.

- Camp Dutch ovens come in a wide range of sizes, from tiny 1-quart models with a diameter of only about 6 inches to 45-quart behemoths sporting lids 22 inches in diameter. Of course, the size of the Dutch oven you'll need depends on the size of the crowd you'll be cooking for. The 12-inch/6-quart oven is arguably the most versatile size and the one most often seen in Scouting. This is the oven type for which most of the recipes in this book were designed, serving 8 to 12 people on average.

- For roasting larger cuts of meat, tall baked goods, or for serving more than a dozen people, the 14-inch/10-quart deep Dutch oven is often a requirement. Several recipes in this book call for an oven of this size. Note that a "deep" Dutch oven typically has an internal depth of at least 5 inches.

- If you do not have an oven of the size discussed above, or if you need to cook for more or fewer people than specified in a given recipe, use the serving and equipment information found in the recipe to scale the number of servings to your specific requirements and available equipment.

- Camp Dutch ovens manufactured from aluminum are often used when equipment weight is a concern, such as on canoe or kayak expeditions, or when the camp cooking is managed by younger Scouts who can't safely handle hefty cookware. Compared to cast iron, the lighter weight of aluminum is a welcome alternative in these situations.

Camp Dutch ovens come in a wide range of sizes to suit your specific requirements. *SCOTT H. SIMERLY SR.*

However, cooking results can vary significantly between cast iron and aluminum ovens. Compared to aluminum, cast iron excels at heat distribution and retention. Aluminum also has a much lower melting temperature than cast iron, important in foul weather because, like a blacksmith's bellows, high wind can greatly raise the temperature of coals. Aluminum ovens can actually sag and melt under these conditions. And aluminum is unable to develop the natural nonstick coating that cast iron can. The recipes in this book have been developed using cast-iron ovens. When using aluminum ovens, bear in mind that actual cooking times may vary from the directions, especially in adverse weather.

Planning for the Obvious . . .
and the Unexpected

- If you are a camp-cooking neophyte, keep your menu simple. Raise the challenge level only after you've become more skilled and confident in your abilities. Taking on more work than one can manage is a common camp kitchen mistake, and the botched meal that results is sure to disappoint not only the one doing the work but also the hungry stomachs depending on the chef.

- Foul weather adds a powerful variable to the camp cooking equation. And bugs and wild animals further distract by keeping you on the defensive. Prior to any outing, weather and critters should be considered and planned for appropriately. Be realistic about what you can handle under the likely circumstances. The more trying the conditions, the simpler the menu should be.

- Divide kitchen duties among Scouts and leaders to lighten the load while cooking and cleaning. Discuss roles and responsibilities in advance so there is no confusion or push-back when it comes time to engage.

- Read through and understand the entire recipe before commencing preparation. By doing so, you will be more efficient in the camp kitchen and less likely to make a critical mistake.

- Be sure that you have everything needed before starting the coals by first gathering all ingredients and cooking utensils to your work area.

- They are often enthusiastic to help, but younger Scouts can require much more supervision. Make sure you can manage the additional workload when assigning tasks to the tenderfoots. Some don't know a can opener from a pizza cutter or won't have a clue as to how to crack an egg.

- The younger the children, the more they tend to openly grumble about their food, even when it is obviously awesome to everyone else. And after a long evening of cooking in camp, complaining is the last thing you want to hear from the Scouts. A powerful way to avoid this is to include your Scouts, especially the younger ones, in the meal-planning process. By giving them a voice, they become stakeholders in the meal's success and are more likely to enjoy, not just tolerate, the results.

- When planning your menu, don't ignore the flexibility of the camp Dutch oven, which can be used in place of a frying pan, grille grate, or cook pot for many recipes that otherwise require them. If a camp stove, barbecue grill, or wood fire will be unavailable for your favorite recipes at your next outing, consider adapting these dishes to the circumstances. A camp Dutch oven and a bag of briquettes can probably do the job easily and admirably.

- Even the most foolproof dish sometimes ends its short life tragically dumped in the dirt by fate or accident. Whatever the cause may be, always have a Plan B at the ready, whether boxed macaroni or a map to the nearest grocery store. At some point, you and your Scouts are likely to need it.

Younger Scouts love helping with the cooking chores, especially when a Dutch oven is in the lineup!
SCOTT H. SIMERLY SR.

Managing the Heat

- Many Dutch oven recipes with a high liquid content, such as stews, can easily tolerate non-exact briquette counts. This means irregular-size coals from the campfire can be readily used as the fuel source instead. By using embers from the campfire, the additional 20 minutes or so required to start briquettes from scratch is eliminated. This also makes many Dutch oven dinner recipes a viable option at lunchtime, even if the schedule is tight.

- Intense heat is transferred through the walls of a Dutch oven in those areas where coals come into *direct contact* with the metal. Food touching the walls on the inside surface of these hot spots will likely char. With coals on the lid, it is imperative that tall foods, such as rising breads or roasts, are cooked in a Dutch oven deep enough for the food to avoid contacting the lid's inside surface. And underneath the oven, the briquettes must be positioned to not directly touch the metal's underside. Otherwise food on the floor of the oven will probably burn. If these simple rules are followed, you should never find it necessary to scrape carbon from your breads or expensive cuts of meat.

- Briquettes often clump together when placing or moving the oven during cooking. They sometimes congregate on the lid, but their sly gatherings usually occur under the oven, where they are more difficult to observe. The problem with this unruly behavior is that it can create hot spots that produce uneven cooking, especially while baking. To prevent this, redistribute the wayward coals as necessary, especially under the oven, and rotate the oven one-quarter turn over the briquettes every 15 minutes or so. At the same time, use a lid-lifter to carefully rotate the lid one-quarter turn relative to the base.

- Heat escapes quickly when the lid is raised from a Dutch oven. Tempting as it may be to continually peek at that cheesecake, don't do so unless absolutely necessary. You'll only lengthen the cooking time.

- Hot briquettes quickly fail when used directly on moist surfaces. Avoid this common mistake by placing your coals and oven on a metal tray or other durable, dry, fireproof surface, such as the flat side of a row of cinder blocks. A tray or hard surface prevents the oven from settling down into the soil and onto direct contact with the coals under the oven, which could otherwise cause the food to char. Cooking on a tray or raised surface also protects the ground from scarring and makes ash cleanup and disposal easier once the coals expire.

- Always bring plenty of extra charcoal briquettes to cover contingencies. Food preparation may take longer than expected, requiring additional coals to complete the meal. Windy, cold, or wet weather can also greatly increase the number of coals required. Don't get caught with an empty bag of briquettes and your food half-baked.

- Preheating the Dutch oven is called for in recipes that require hot metal to properly kick-start the cooking process, such as when sautéing vegetables, browning meats, and baking. An exact coal count isn't essential for preheating the oven, with about two dozen briquettes generally adequate for the job. When browning or sautéing, all the coals go under the oven because the lid is unused. When preheating the oven for recipes requiring the lid, the coals should be distributed between the lid and under the oven. Use any unspent coals for subsequent cooking steps.

- Most recipes from the Dutch oven are remarkably resilient against overcooking. The heavy, tight-fitting lid helps trap moisture, which prevents foods from drying out when left on the coals longer than they need to be. However, as is true in the home kitchen, baked items from the Dutch oven require more precision for great results. So pay closer attention to temperature and timing when baking.

- When cooking with more than one Dutch oven at mealtime, stacking the ovens, one on top of the other, can be a useful technique if the cooking area is limited. This method also saves on briquettes, as the coals on the lid of the bottom oven also heat the bottom of the

Efficiency can be maximized by stacking Dutch ovens when more than one is being used to prepare the meal. *TIM CONNERS*

oven on top. But be aware that stacking complicates the preparation, requiring careful placement of the ovens and more attention to coal distribution and cooking times. For instance, you wouldn't want to place a dish that requires frequent stirring at the bottom of the stack. Nor would you stack a Dutch oven that uses a low coal count on top of one requiring a lot of briquettes. Stacking several ovens can also be more hazardous, as a taller tower becomes more prone to toppling. Plan carefully and be extra cautious when using stacks.

Dealing with the Weather

- When a coal-covered lid is lifted while the wind is stirring, or if the lid is bumped while lifting, you'll watch in helpless wonder as ash majestically floats down onto your food. It's a beautiful sight, like powdered sugar on a chocolate cake. Unfortunately, ash doesn't taste like powdered sugar. So avoid jarring the lid when lifting, and remove it immediately toward the downwind side. This will minimize your ash-to-food ratio.

- In very windy conditions, place the Dutch oven behind a windscreen of some sort while cooking; otherwise, the coals will quickly erode and the food will be subjected to uneven heating, potentially burned in some areas and undercooked in others. A row of coolers or storage bins can serve handily as a windbreak. Dutch oven stands, purpose-built for cooking off the ground, often come with built-in windscreens.

- Perhaps the most challenging of all outdoor cooking situations involves rain. Talk about the feeling of desperation when a downpour suddenly develops over your camp kitchen just as you pour hot coals on the lid of your Dutch oven. Large sheets of heavy-duty aluminum foil, tented loosely over the top of the oven and tray, can offer some protection in a pinch but are unlikely to shield completely during a cloudburst. A large barbecue grill with a lid can protect your oven from the rain, with a metal tray placed on the grill grate serving as the cook surface. And, once again, a Dutch oven stand with a windscreen would serve nicely, with the screen supporting sheets of heavy foil or a tray for keeping the rain off the coals. If there is no other option, cooking can also be conducted under a table, picnic or folding, the table top covered with a plastic sheet to keep rain from making its way underneath. It is imperative in this situation that the cook not huddle under the table with the oven because of the danger of asphyxiation from the burning coals.

- A camp kitchen tent is arguably the most comfortable option for cooking with a Dutch oven in wet weather, but good judgment is a must when choosing and using a kitchen tent because of the very real risk of asphyxiation and fire. See the previous section for important information on kitchen tent safety.

- Cooking with a Dutch oven in snow presents its own unique difficulties, but these are easily managed if planned for in advance. If the snow is deep and cannot be easily cleared, cook off the ground on a durable surface. For example, a metal tray on a concrete picnic table would work well in this instance. A Dutch oven stand can also be very useful in the snow. If your camping area has a sturdy grill, a

Dutch ovens do the job even in deep snow! *FRONTIER FREEDOM—JENNY LAMB, ALASKA*

tray placed on the grate can be used. Wood logs can also be arranged in the snow to securely support a metal tray for placing the Dutch oven. The flat surface of several cinder blocks would also work well in this situation.

Making the Impossible Easy

- The camp Dutch oven is a remarkably versatile cooking device. It excels at allowing the heat source to be placed where it is needed most. With the lid off and briquettes underneath, the Dutch oven, or the inside surface of its lid, makes a fine skillet for many foods. With the lid on and the coals distributed so that most are on top, it becomes an outstanding baking device for corn bread and cakes. Dividing the coals more evenly between lid and bottom produces an ideal cooking environment for recipes that contain or produce a lot of liquid, such as stews and roasts. And using indirect heating by surrounding only the base with a ring of coals, even delicate dishes, prone to burning, can be prepared.

- The seasoned walls of a cast-iron Dutch oven carry a flavor that's a collection of everything cooked prior and which can transfer to everything prepared after. For most savory dishes, this is a unique and complementary flavor, a signature hallmark of Dutch oven cooking. However, for some desserts or recipes with a more delicate taste, the additional flavor can be unwanted. Consider using heavy-duty aluminum foil lining for these types of recipes to minimize flavor transfer from the walls of the oven.

- Heavy-duty aluminum foil, used as a liner during cooking, can be grabbed at the corners to lift and transport stiff foods, such as breads and cakes, from oven to the serving table. This handy technique avoids the need to move the heavy oven. But do not attempt to use this technique with gloppy or runny foods. If the foil would rupture in doing so, you could find your skin covered in scalding, sticky goo.

- Standard-depth ovens, shallow compared to their "deep" counterparts, are generally preferable for baking low-rise items like biscuits and corn breads. Because the lid's heat source is closer to the dough, better top-browning results.

- A trivet is a three-point base that provides an insulating gap between a hot cooking surface and the tray, pie pan, or cake pan placed on it. The trivet is used to prevent sensitive foods from burning. These can be purchased commercially but are also easily fashioned from a trio of marble-size balls of foil or small pebbles placed directly on the inside bottom of the Dutch oven.

- The Dutch oven makes for a fantastic roaster. Not only do meats become fork-tender when cooked low and slow in the oven, but so do vegetables, especially roots and tubers such as carrots and sweet potatoes.

- As multitalented as cast-iron Dutch ovens are, they do not excel at making hot beverages. Some of the oily coating will be released when water is boiled in a Dutch oven. The greasy, brownish-colored liquid that results is not well-suited to a great cup of coffee or tea. If you are in need of pure hot water, use a clean standard cook pot instead.

Cleaning Up

- A lining of heavy-duty foil in the Dutch oven is excellent for containing mess from gooey recipes. Once the foil is removed following the meal, most of the glop goes with it, making cleanup much easier. Note that foil is not suitable for recipes that require a lot of stirring, because the foil can snag and tear.

- It is a common belief that a lining of aluminum foil is necessary to prevent foods from baking to the interior of a Dutch oven. The reality is that virtually no food will strongly adhere to the walls of well-seasoned cast iron. In these circumstances, save your foil and let your oven's natural nonstick surface do its work.

- A pair of large butler basins or storage containers, one filled with cleaning water, the other with rinse water, makes cleanup more efficient.

• Cleaning greasy cookware and dishes with cold water can be a real challenge to one's patience. Use warm water to cut grease and make cleanup more rapid and hygienic. Place a pot of water over the stove or campfire to warm for this purpose while the meal is being served. The water will

Lining Dutch ovens with aluminum foil.
SCOTT H. SIMERLY SR.

be hot once it's time for cleanup. Carefully pour the hot water into the wash bin, bringing it to a safe temperature with cold water as required.

• Use dishwashing liquid sparingly during cleanup, just enough to do the job. Only detergents that are biodegradable should be used outdoors. As a general rule, however, avoid using detergents on cast iron. See the next section for the reason why.

• Dirty dishes left to lie will eventually attract bugs and wild animals. To avoid such interest, ensure that all cookware and utensils have been washed and rinsed before leaving camp during the day or when retiring for the evening.

• Dispose of wash and rinse water, also called "gray water," in a manner acceptable for your particular camp. Some camping areas have dedicated gray water disposal stations. Never dump gray water directly into a stream or lake.

Information specific to cleaning and storing cast iron can be found in the following section.

CARING FOR YOUR DUTCH OVEN

Its reputation for longevity didn't come by accident or mistake, so don't waste time pampering your cast-iron Dutch oven. It will prove to be exceptionally durable cookware if only a few simple rules are followed: 1) avoid using metal scrub pads or detergent when cleaning; 2) don't pour cool water onto hot cast iron; and 3) be careful not to strike your oven on a hard surface. Do these, and your Dutch oven will easily last many generations.

Cast iron's nonstick coating, also called its "patina" or "seasoning," does not come from man-made chemicals. It builds naturally through the cooking process. When wiped with cooking oil before each use, the microporosity within the cast iron traps and holds the oil, which then hardens under the heat of cooking into a sterile layer with excellent nonstick properties. With a little care both before and after cooking, your cast iron's patina will retain its durable and slippery nature indefinitely.

The following sections provide tips on properly caring for your Dutch oven and what to do if your cast iron's natural nonstick coating is inadvertently damaged or removed.

Cleaning and Storing a Dutch Oven

- For cleanup, a cast-iron Dutch oven requires no more than a sponge or dish rag for wiping, a gentle nonmetallic scrub pad or spatula for scraping, warm water for washing, plenty of clean water for rinsing, and a towel for drying. Metal scouring pads are a sure way to destroy your Dutch oven's coating, and should never be used. Detergents should be avoided unless absolutely necessary because soap attacks the cast iron's patina.

- The warmer the wash water, the more effectively that grease can be cut by water alone. When grease is heavy or solidified, and the wash water cold, a *very small* amount of dish soap will make Dutch oven cleanup easier. But the outer layer of patina can be compromised in the process. For this reason, use soap sparingly, if ever.

- Never use a dishwasher to clean your cast-iron Dutch oven. The strong detergents in a dishwasher can remove so much coating that re-seasoning would be required.

- Some dishes will challenge even the best nonstick coating, especially if the food is frozen when first placed in the Dutch oven, or if the food is accidentally charred while cooking. Soaking cookware in water is the usual remedy for tough stuck-on foods, but cast iron should not be left to soak for long periods in plain water. Otherwise, the patina may weaken and rust spots form. Instead, an effective and non-damaging cleaning method is to pour an inch or two of very hot water into the soiled oven before the residue has a chance to harden. Then place the lid on. The residue will begin to loosen after just a few minutes. Once the soak water cools to a safe temperature, the residue can be removed with a nonmetallic spatula or scrub pad and the oven then cleaned and rinsed as usual.

A big basin with a lot of water makes washing a Dutch oven much easier. SCOTT H. SIMERLY SR.

- If a separate cook pot is unavailable to heat wash water, the soiled Dutch oven itself can be used by adding a couple of inches of clean water then placing it over the camp fire or any remaining hot coals. Once the water is hot, very carefully move the oven to a safe location. Placing the lid on prior to moving will help prevent scalding water from sloshing onto unprotected skin. Once the metal cools to a temperature safe for cleaning, the food residue will have loosened and subsequent cleanup will be much easier.

• When cleaning or drying, never allow a Dutch oven to go completely dry over a fire. The cast iron won't melt or warp, but the patina can quickly turn to ash without the protective influence of the moisture.

• Avoid placing very hot cast iron in cool water. The resulting thermal shock may warp or crack the metal. Wait for your cookware to cool to the touch before immersing or pouring in wash water.

• Rub or spray a thin layer of food-grade oil over the entire surface of your cookware, including the legs and handles, both before using and after each cleaning. Doing so before cooking will further build the durability and effectiveness of the nonstick coating. And doing so after cleaning will protect the patina and prevent rust during storage. Using paper towels to spread the oil makes the job easier and less messy.

Recoating a camp Dutch oven with vegetable oil.
TIM CONNERS

• Vegetable oil can be used to protect your cookware prior to short-term storage. But over long periods of time, vegetable oils may turn rancid and gummy. Especially avoid coating the metal with lard or other animal-based fats prior to storage, as these are more likely to putrefy. For long storage periods, a very thin coat of food-grade mineral oil is a better option as it will neither gum up nor turn rancid. If mineral oil has been applied, wipe the surface of the oven with a paper towel immediately prior to next use.

- Store your Dutch oven with the lid slightly ajar to provide fresh air and continuous ventilation to the oven's interior. A folded paper towel placed in the bottom of the oven during storage will soak up excess oil and moisture and will delay or prevent gumming of vegetable oils protecting the oven's walls.

- If cast iron has an Achilles heel, it is its slightly brittle nature. This isn't a threat in the home kitchen. In fact, care must be taken to prevent your heavy Dutch oven from damaging your sinks, countertops, floors, and cabinets. Outdoors can be found the Dutch oven's only true nemesis: bare concrete or rock surfaces. Banging or dropping your oven or lid against concrete picnic tables and walkways or large boulders, even against each other, can fracture the cast iron if the impact is severe. Take extra care when moving and storing your cast iron in the home kitchen, during transportation, and when outdoors around hard surfaces.

The Challenging Life of Your Oven's Nonstick Coating

Cast iron's nonstick patina is reasonably durable considering that it forms naturally from food oils and not man-made chemicals. But with heavy use and less than ideal cleaning and maintenance, the outer layers of the seasoning can disappear in sporadic patches. Don't be overly concerned if a similar situation occurs with your oven. Losing patina in small patches or rings has minimal effect on the overall nonstick properties of the oven, and those areas from which patina is lost will immediately begin forming new layers with subsequent use. Your cast iron may occasionally lose its showcase black luster. But looks can be deceiving. Your cast iron will perform well regardless, provided that it continues to be well oiled before and after each use.

Here are some additional tips for preserving your Dutch oven's prized seasoning.

- Cooking highly acidic foods, such as tomato sauces, will sometimes remove what at first appears to be an alarming amount of patina. But, again, this situation can look worse than it really is, as usually only the outermost layers of seasoning are lost. The tougher, inner layers are left behind, and the nonstick and protective properties of the seasoning remain. So don't hesitate to cook acidic foods in your Dutch oven. But do give your oven an occasional break from foods that attack the patina to allow the seasoning layers to rebuild.

- Because Dutch ovens retain heat long after the oven is removed from the coals, provided that the lid is used, meals can proceed at a more leisurely pace, even in cooler weather. So it isn't unusual for foods to rest, covered, in the Dutch oven for an hour or more after cooking. But it isn't advisable to allow foods to remain for much longer than this because the patina can eventually weaken through long-term contact with the food. Take your time with your meal, but soon afterward, move the leftovers to the ice chest and then wash the oven.

- Use a long-handled wooden or silicone spoon for mixing and stirring in your Dutch oven. Occasional use of metal spoons is acceptable, but avoid sustained use of metal utensils, which can scratch the patina.

If the surface of typical nonstick kitchen cookware is damaged or begins to peel away, it is usually ruined. Man-made nonstick surfaces can not be easily repaired nor is the peeling material safe for consumption. In contrast, the beauty of cast iron patina is that it can be easily repaired if damaged. It is also a safe material, forming naturally from foods, so flaking patina does not jeopardize health. You will *never* have to discard cast iron simply because patina is lost or damaged.

There are some situations, however, when the patina can be so damaged that a full re-seasoning of the Dutch oven is the best approach for restoring the natural protective layer. Heavy damage to the patina can occur suddenly when a Dutch oven is inadvertently left over very hot flames or coals and the food inside completely dries and burns. Large loss of patina can also happen through improper cleaning using harsh detergents or metal scrub pads. But it can also occur insidiously over time if the cast iron's surface isn't re-oiled before and after each meal.

One telltale sign that it is time to re-season the oven is the loss of nonstick properties over much of the cast iron's surface. And you can be certain that the protective layer is completely missing in areas

Close-up of cast iron with damaged patina. *TIM CONNERS*

where large amounts of rust are seen. No worries, though. Re-seasoning is an easy process and is discussed next.

Re-seasoning Your Oven

The process of seasoning a Dutch oven is straightforward and involves little more than baking a layer of cooking oil onto the surface of the cast iron in a hot grill or kitchen oven. These steps explain the process in detail.

1. Use a metal scrub pad or steel wool to remove rust spots and damaged regions of patina. Scrub the entire surface of the oven if the situation warrants it. When re-seasoning, err on the side of removing too much patina. The new seasoned surface will be more uniform in strength and appearance as a result.

2. Thoroughly wash the cast iron, completely dry with a towel, then allow to air-dry for an additional hour or two. The surface must be free of all moisture before the next step.

3. Wipe a layer of cooking oil over the entire surface of the Dutch oven, both inside and out. Don't forget to do the same with the lid. Either solid shortening that has been melted or liquid oil can be used.

4. Place the cookware upside down on the rack of a barbecue grill or kitchen oven. Tilt the base of the Dutch oven, propping it at an angle with a heat-safe utensil. Lean the lid against the base, the flanged top facing downward. Excess oil forms sticky patches wherever it pools on the surface. By leaning the base and lid of the oven, excess oil will drain from the surface.

5. In a kitchen oven, place a large sheet of aluminum foil on a rack under the cast iron to catch dripping oil.

6. Close the oven door or grill lid and bring to medium heat, about 350°F to 400°F. The oil will smoke slightly and, for some, may smell disagreeable. This is

Camp Dutch oven base and lid arranged on the grill for re-seasoning. *TIM CONNERS*

normal and shouldn't be a problem when using a grill outdoors. But smoke and odor can be an issue in the home kitchen, especially if a smoke alarm is in the vicinity. In this case, use the grill option instead.

7. Bake the cast iron for at least 1 hour. Smoking will probably have abated by then; if not, continue to bake until no more smoke is seen.

8. Allow cast iron to cool completely before removing from the oven or grill.

9. Your cookware's new seasoned coating may be shiny dark brown instead of black. This is especially true for cast iron seasoned for the first time. The brownish color has no bearing on nonstick performance and will eventually toughen with use into a deep black.

A layer of patina is sometimes baked onto the cast iron at the factory. But if your new cast iron arrives bare naked, a gunmetal gray, it will require seasoning before first use. Just follow the directions above, and don't neglect step one. The metal may appear to not need scrubbing, but unseasoned cast iron usually has an invisible wax-like coating applied to prevent rusting on the way to the store. Use hot water and a thorough scrubbing with a stiff metal pad or brush to remove this coating before moving on to step two.

IMPORTANT ACCESSORIES FOR DUTCH OVEN COOKING

The Dutch oven may be the star of the show, but you'll need to gather a few additional items for preparing the heat source and, more importantly, for safely managing the oven and coals once they are hot.

- **Charcoal.** For your fuel source, use a high-quality briquette of standard size. Extra large or small briquettes, even embers from the camp fire, can also work, but their nonstandard size will make it more challenging to achieve proper results when following a cookbook, such as this one, that specifies exact coal counts based on the standard briquette size. Carry plenty of extra coal for contingencies.

- **Coal Starter.** A batch of hot coals can be started using briquette lighter fluid, but a less messy and more rapid approach is to use a chimney coal starter. These are safe, simple, and inexpensive devices, and a necessity in some regions where lighter fluid is banned. Coals are loaded in the top of a cylindrical metal canister, about 1 foot in height. A compartment at the bottom of the canister is used to burn a small amount of crumpled paper, and the rising flames ignite the briquettes in the upper chimney. Vents cut in the side draw air into the cylinder, accelerating the ignition of the coals. Once the briquettes ash over, usually after about 20 minutes, they are ready to be poured from the chimney using a handle on the side.

Typical camp Dutch oven equipment, including lifter being used to raise lid from the oven. *TIM CONNERS*

37

- **Coal Tray.** Many areas, otherwise safe for cooking, may not be suitable for cooking directly on the bare ground, either because of excessive soil moisture or because doing so could scar a sensitive surface. Avoid these problems by using a metal platter, such as an inexpensive pizza tray. A tray also makes ash cleanup less messy. Select a coal tray at least as wide as the maximum width of the oven.

- **Tongs.** Long-handled metal barbecue tongs are necessary for properly distributing hot briquettes on, under, and around the oven. Sturdy tongs with good gripping capability and a handle length of at least 1 foot are recommended.

- **Heavy Gloves.** These are absolutely necessary for protecting your hands and forearms when handling coals, removing the lid, or transporting a hot Dutch oven by the bail handle. Choose thick, long leather barbecue gloves that extend well up the arm. Avoid fabric kitchen mitts, which won't fully protect against searing heat and which can catch fire around hot coals. Also avoid silicone mitts, which are stiff and awkward to use.

Arranging coals on the lid of a camp Dutch oven. Heavy leather gloves are important for protecting the skin from burns. *TIM CONNERS*

- **Lid Lifter.** This device firmly grips and safely removes the hot, heavy, coal-covered lid from a Dutch oven. Made for this purpose, lifters are safer and more stable than using makeshift items out of the tool box.

Coal starters, tongs, and barbecue gloves can be found at larger grocery stores in the seasonal section. Lid lifters are available in well-stocked outdoor cooking departments of hardware stores and super-centers and can also be ordered online. Camp Dutch ovens are often stocked by outfitters and outdoor retailers. Use Web-based search engines to find those closest to you. There are also many sources online, some of which are listed in Appendix B.

STEP-BY-STEP DUTCH OVEN TUTORIAL

This section will take the new outdoor chef step by step through a great-tasting camp Dutch oven recipe. If you're new to Dutch oven cooking, follow this tutorial from start to finish. You'll find the process easy and enjoyable. Afterward, you'll be ready to jump into any of the other terrific recipes that await in the following pages.

The hearty recipe used here, *2x4 Soup,* is adapted from *The Scout's Outdoor Cookbook,* and is famous for its simple preparation, easy cleanup, and outstanding results. It serves 8 to 10 people and takes less than an hour to prepare.

2x4 Soup

First, gather the ingredients you'll need from the grocery store:

About 2 pounds lean ground beef (the weight doesn't need to be exact for this recipe, but to avoid an unhealthy and greasy mess, make sure that the beef is lean)

2 (10½-ounce) cans condensed vege-table soup, such as Campbell's brand (the details with the soup are important for this recipe: it must be *condensed,* and it will say so on the label)

Preparing stew in a camp Dutch oven. SCOTT H. SIMERLY SR.

2 (10-ounce) cans diced tomatoes and green chilies, such as Ro-Tel brand

2 (15-ounce) cans pinto beans, such as Bush's brand

Now is also the time to gather your cooking equipment, if you haven't already done so:

12-inch / 6-quart Dutch oven, preseasoned and oiled

Long-handled tongs

Long-sleeve leather barbecue gloves

Metal platter, such as a pizza tray

Chimney charcoal starter

A few sheets of newspaper

Lighter

Standard-size charcoal briquettes, such as Kingsford brand

Long-handled wooden spoon

Long-handled serving ladle

Serving bowls, spoons, and napkins or paper towels

Sponge, soap, and drying towel

Can opener

Hand sanitizer

Pack all the gear for the road; before leaving home, make sure that the ground beef is tightly sealed in a container or ziplock bag then placed on ice in a good quality cooler until it is ready to be used at camp. Avoid potentially cross-contaminating raw fruits, vegetables, cheese, beverages, drinking ice, and the like by keeping meat in a cooler separate from these items.

Once at camp, prepare the coals by pouring about 2 dozen briquettes into the chimney starter. Place the metal tray in a fire-safe area of the camp, preferably on rock, gravel, or bare earth. The cooking surface must be durable.

Be safe. Cook well away from combustibles such as dry grass, trees, or wooden structures. Notify the Scouts to stay clear of the cooking area because of the danger of hot coals on the ground.

Place the chimney starter on the metal tray. Loosely wad a sheet of newspaper, insert it into the bottom chamber of the chimney starter, and ignite the paper.

The coal should begin to burn on its edges within the starter. Indication will be subtle at first: perhaps a small amount of smoke coming from the chimney after the main fire from the paper dies down. The smoke from the coals should grow in intensity as the minutes pass. If not, burn more paper under the coals until they begin to smoke more aggressively.

About 20 minutes after the coals begin to smoke, they will be ready to use for cooking, although the precise time depends on the design of the chimney starter and wind and weather. The briquettes in the bottom of the chimney starter will be red-hot, the ones at the top partially ashed over (but well on their way to red-hot as well). Waiting until the top coals are fully ashed over is unnecessary.

With protective gloves on your hands, pour all the coals onto the tray and place the camp Dutch oven over the briquettes. Using tongs, move the coals so that all are distributed evenly under the oven. Allow the Dutch oven to warm for about 5 minutes.

Thoroughly wash your hands then place the ground beef into the Dutch oven. *Immediately* after you've handled the raw ground beef, and *before* touching any other cooking instruments or ingredients, use sanitizer or soap and water to clean your hands once again. (If you've ever had food poisoning, you'll have the experience to know why this step is so important.)

If the oven is fully preheated, you'll be greeted by some excellent sizzle. If not, don't worry. The oven will be very hot soon enough, and the meat will eventually brown regardless. Break up clumps of meat with the wooden spoon, and occasionally stir. Enjoy the aroma!

Once the meat is thoroughly browned (actually, it will probably look more gray in color), *and with no trace of pink remaining,* pour the contents of the two cans of soup and the two cans of tomatoes and chilies over the meat in the oven. Discard the juice from the two cans of pinto beans and pour the beans into the oven. Stir well with the wooden spoon.

Warm the ingredients over the coals. All have been previously cooked by this point, so a sterilizing simmer is unnecessary. 2x4 is ready to serve once hot. Note that the lid to the Dutch oven is not required.

With gloves on your hands, *very carefully* carry the hot oven using the bail handle to a sturdy, heat-proof table or platform. Use the ladle to serve.

Congratulations! You've prepared your first camp Dutch oven recipe.

But the work isn't over yet. The hot coals back on the tray still present a potential hazard, and the cooking area must be kept safe until the coals expire. Be diligent. After the coals have fully cooled, discard the ash in an appropriate fire-safe manner.

Enjoy your meal, then place any leftovers in a food-safe container on ice in a cooler. Dutch ovens are usually very easy to clean when used to cook stews and soups. You'll find this recipe is no exception.

Once the cast iron is no longer hot to the touch, the oven can be rinsed. An initial wash using a small amount of water will remove most food particles. The oven can then be placed in a bin of clean warm water or run under the faucet, using a dish sponge inside and out to finish. No soap should be used on the cast iron because detergent can damage the nonstick coating. However, you'll need soapy water to clean the wooden spoon and ladle.

Thoroughly dry the oven then re-coat the surface, inside and out, with a light layer of vegetable oil using a paper towel. Set the oven aside until it's time for your next cooking masterpiece.

The recipe for **2x4 Soup** comes from Roberta Kleinik, Advancement Chair for Troop 131 in Jacksonville, Florida.

The Commissioner's French Toast

"This is my favorite Dutch oven breakfast recipe. It's quick to prepare and easy to clean up. And it tastes great on cold mornings. Come to think of it, it's great even on mornings that aren't so cold."

PREPARATION AT CAMP:

1. Line the Dutch oven with aluminum foil and grease the foil.

2. Whisk eggs in a large mixing bowl.

3. Spread half of the bread pieces in Dutch oven then cover with cubed cream cheese.

4. Layer the remainder of the bread in the oven and pour the eggs over everything.

5. Sprinkle all with cinnamon.

6. Bake for about 30 minutes using 17 coals on the lid and 8 briquettes under the oven, until a knife or toothpick comes out clean.

7. Serve with syrup.

REQUIRED EQUIPMENT:

12-inch Dutch oven
Large mixing bowl
Heavy-duty aluminum foil

Keith Huffstetler, Winston-Salem, North Carolina
District Commissioner and Committee Chair
Troop 934, Piedmont District, Old Hickory Council

1 dozen eggs

1 (1-pound) loaf sliced bread, torn into cubes

8 ounces cream cheese, cubed into small pieces

1 teaspoon ground cinnamon

1 (12-ounce) bottle pancake syrup

Servings: 6–8
Preparation Time: 1 hour
Challenge Level: Easy

Fombelina Sticky Rolls

1 (1-pound) loaf frozen bread dough, thawed

Butter to grease pan

½ cup packed brown sugar

1 (3.4-ounce) package regular vanilla pudding mix

½ teaspoon ground cinnamon

¼ cup nuts or raisins (optional)

¼ cup (½ standard stick) butter, melted

1 tablespoon milk

TIP: Steps 1 through 5 can be completed the evening before baking. Store dough, covered and chilled in the cooler, until ready to use in the morning.

Servings: 6–8
Preparation Time: 1¼ hours
Challenge Level: Easy

"Fombelina Sticky Rolls was adapted from a recipe given to me by Cindy Blaine, a longtime staff member at the now-closed Girl Scout Camp Fombelina, in Fombell, Pennsylvania. When we stayed at the camp's lodge, my Girl Scout troop used to make *huge* trays of 'Cindy's Sticky Buns' on Sunday mornings. We prepared the rolls the evening before, stored them overnight in the fridge, then baked them in the morning while we packed and cleaned the lodge. They were great motivation for getting the work done. When my son became a Boy Scout, so did Mom. A few years ago, I adapted Cindy's recipe for the camp Dutch oven because Boy Scouts usually don't stay in lodges with electric ovens. The Scouts can't believe the rolls are so easy to make, and the Scoutmasters are always thrilled to have them with their morning coffee."

PREPARATION AT CAMP:

1. Tear half of bread loaf into small, nickel-size dough balls and place in greased cake pan.

2. Sprinkle brown sugar, pudding mix, cinnamon, and optional nuts or raisins over dough balls.

3. Mix melted butter with milk and pour over the pieces in the cake pan.

4. Tear remaining bread loaf into small dough balls and scatter over the top of the previous pieces.

5. Cover pan and allow dough to rise for about 45 minutes, or until the bread roughly doubles in size.

6. Place pan on trivet in preheated Dutch oven. Using 17 coals on the lid and 8 briquettes under the oven, bake for about 30 minutes, until the top of the dough is golden brown.

7. Remove cake pan from oven and carefully turn sticky rolls onto a large plate or tray. Serve warm.

REQUIRED EQUIPMENT:

12-inch camp Dutch oven with trivet
9-inch-diameter round cake pan

Jo Posluszny, Scranton, Pennsylvania
Committee Member
Troop 251, Northeastern Pennsylvania Council

Ol' Strasbourg Onion Pie

"Friends from France served this dish to me while I was stationed there in 2000."

PREPARATION AT CAMP:

1. Melt butter in skillet and sauté the onions until translucent.

2. Add the bacon to onion in the skillet and cook until crisp.

3. Mix flour with bacon and onion in the skillet and remove from heat.

4. Blend sour cream with eggs in a medium-size bowl. Add bacon-onion mixture to bowl and stir well.

5. Pour mixture into pie crust and place on trivet in Dutch oven.

6. Using 17 coals on the lid and 8 briquettes under the oven, bake for 45 minutes or until knife inserted in middle comes out clean. Refresh coals as required.

7. Add salt and black pepper to taste.

REQUIRED EQUIPMENT:

12-inch camp Dutch oven with trivet
Medium-size skillet
Medium-size mixing bowl

Delano LaGow, Oswego, Illinois
Committee Member
Troop 31, Three Fires Council

¼ cup (½ standard stick) butter

1 pound sweet onion, diced

2 strips bacon, diced

1 tablespoon all-purpose flour

¼ cup sour cream

4 eggs, beaten

1 (9-inch) premade frozen pie crust with foil pan, thawed

Salt and ground black pepper to taste

Servings: 6–8
Preparation Time: 1¼ hours
Challenge Level: Moderate

1 pound frozen shredded hash browns

2 tablespoons butter, cut into several pats

½ teaspoon salt

⅛ teaspoon ground black pepper

1 cup imitation crab meat, broken into small pieces

6 eggs

1 cup heavy cream

½ cup sour cream

⅛ teaspoon ground cayenne pepper

¼ teaspoon onion powder

¼ teaspoon garlic powder

1 cup shredded mozzarella cheese

6 jumbo shrimp (optional)

½ cup grated Parmesan cheese

⅛ teaspoon paprika

Options: Many interesting ingredients can be substituted for the imitation crab meat: real crab, chopped scallops, shrimp, sausage, ham, or Canadian bacon. Hard cheeses, such as Asiago, can also be added.

Servings: 6–8
Preparation Time: 1½ hours
Challenge Level: Moderate

Breakfast Seafood Frittata

"This recipe was created to challenge Scouts to expand their cooking repertoire on campouts, to go beyond simple cobblers and stews. There will be no problem rousing the boys from slumber with Breakfast Seafood Frittata, which was awarded third place in the entree category in *Scouting* magazine's 2009 Great Tastes in Camp Cooking contest."

PREPARATION AT CAMP:

1. Coat 10-inch-diameter cake pan with vegetable oil or nonstick cooking spray.

2. Evenly line pan with hash browns.

3. Arrange butter pats over hash browns and sprinkle with salt and black pepper.

4. Layer about a quarter of the imitation crab meat over top of hash browns.

5. In a medium-size bowl, whisk together the eggs, heavy cream, and sour cream. Add cayenne pepper, onion powder, garlic powder, and remaining imitation crab meat. Mix well and pour over crab and hash browns in cake pan.

6. Spread mozzarella cheese over egg mixture in pan, adding optional shrimp at this time, arranging each piece like spokes in a wheel.

7. Sprinkle all with Parmesan cheese and paprika.

8. Place cake pan on a trivet in Dutch oven. Cook about 40 minutes, using 15 coals on the lid and 15 briquettes under the oven.

9. Move Dutch oven from coals and remove lid. Set aside, allowing frittata to finish setting.

10. Full firmness should be reached in less than 30 minutes after removing from coals. The dish is ready to serve once an inserted knife comes out clean.

REQUIRED EQUIPMENT:
12-inch camp Dutch oven with trivet
10-inch-diameter round cake pan
Medium-size mixing bowl

Mark F. Schlenker, Indianola, Iowa
Assistant Scoutmaster
Troop 123, Mid-Iowa Council

Breakfast in Bread

PREPARATION AT CAMP:

1. Preheat Dutch oven with 21 coals on the lid and 11 briquettes under the oven.

2. While oven is heating, cleanly slice the top from the rounded bread loaf. Remove the interior of the loaf without breaking the crust. Likewise, remove soft bread from the bread crust "lid." The intent is to make a large bread bowl.

3. In a medium-size mixing bowl, whisk eggs, Spam, bell pepper, tomato, mushrooms, and olives.

4. Melt butter in frying pan over medium heat and scramble the egg mixture until eggs are fully cooked.

5. Cover the bottom of the bread bowl with 1 cup of the shredded cheese.

6. Fill the bread bowl with the egg mixture then add the remaining shredded cheese to the top. Replace bread lid.

7. Place bread on top of trivet in the oven.

8. With coal distribution unchanged, bake for approximately 45 minutes, refreshing coals as required.

9. Remove bread bowl from oven then set aside to cool slightly before cutting into slices.

REQUIRED EQUIPMENT:

Deep 14-inch camp Dutch oven with trivet
Medium-size frying pan
Medium-size mixing bowl

Delano LaGow, Oswego, Illinois
Committee Member
Troop 31, Three Fires Council

1 (24-ounce) loaf round sourdough bread

6 eggs

1 (7-ounce) can Spam, cubed

¼ bell pepper, diced

1 medium tomato, diced

1 (7-ounce) can sliced mushrooms, drained

1 (2¼-ounce) can sliced ripe olives, drained

1 tablespoon butter

6 ounces (1½ cups) shredded cheddar Jack cheese

Servings: 6–8
Preparation Time: 1½ hours
Challenge Level: Moderate

1 pound ground country (breakfast) sausage

8 slices white bread, cubed or torn

6 ounces (1½ cups) shredded cheddar cheese

6 eggs

2 cups milk

1 teaspoon mustard powder

½ teaspoon salt

Dash garlic powder

Dash ground black pepper

Maple syrup or your favorite condiments (optional)

Ray's World-Famous Dutch Oven Breakfast Casserole

PREPARATION AT CAMP:

1. Preheat Dutch oven over 25 coals.

2. Brown sausage, drain grease, and set meat aside.

3. Place bread pieces or cubes in the bottom of Dutch oven.

4. Spoon cooked meat evenly over the bread then sprinkle with cheddar cheese.

5. In a medium-size mixing bowl, beat together eggs, milk, mustard powder, salt, garlic powder, and black pepper.

6. Pour mixture over the bread, sausage, and cheese layers.

7. Bake for 1 hour using 17 coals on the lid and 8 briquettes under the oven. Refresh coals as required.

8. Serve with optional maple syrup or other favorite condiments.

REQUIRED EQUIPMENT:

12-inch camp Dutch oven
Medium-size mixing bowl

Ray McCune, Fort Wayne, Indiana
Committee Member
Troop 344, Anthony Wayne Area Council

Servings: 6–8
Preparation Time: 1¾ hours
Challenge Level: Easy

If it has bacon in it, it has to be good!
CHRISTINE CONNERS

Baloo's Cinnamon Blueberry Crumble

"I made this for the annual Dutch oven cook-off that our Pack participates in and won first place for desserts. There are never any leftovers with this recipe."

PREPARATION AT CAMP:

1. Arrange refrigerated rolls in Dutch oven.

2. Spread blueberry pie filling over and in between rolls.

3. In a small mixing bowl, combine butter, flour, brown sugar, and pecans. Sprinkle mixture over pie filling.

4. Bake for 45 to 50 minutes using 17 coals on the lid and 8 briquettes under the oven, refreshing coals as required.

5. Remove from heat and, while still warm, drizzle rolls with the cream cheese frosting found in the refrigerated roll containers.

REQUIRED EQUIPMENT:
12-inch camp Dutch oven
Small mixing bowl

Tracy Tuttle, Boise, Idaho
Den Leader
Pack 97, Ore-Ida Council

2 (12.4-ounce) containers Pillsbury refrigerated Cinnamon Rolls with Cream Cheese Icing

1 (21-ounce) can blueberry pie filling

¼ cup (½ standard stick) butter, softened

½ cup all-purpose flour

½ cup brown sugar

1 cup chopped pecans

TIP:
Makes a great dessert too.

Servings: 8 (2 rolls each)
Preparation Time: 1¼ hours
Challenge Level: Easy

Quick Dutch Oven Doughnuts

4 cups vegetable oil

2 (12-ounce) containers Pillsbury refrigerated biscuits

½ cup confectioners' sugar

Options: Coat doughnuts in frosting and sprinkles or roll them in cinnamon sugar.

Caution: Hot oil can splatter and burn unprotected skin. Wear clothing that fully protects your arms and legs whenever deep frying.

"These will disappear faster than you can cook them!"

PREPARATION AT CAMP:

1. Heat vegetable oil in Dutch oven over 30 coals.

2. While oil is heating, break each biscuit into 4 separate pieces then roll each piece into a small ball.

3. Test to see if the oil is ready by dropping a very small piece of dough into the oil. If the dough bubbles and begins to fry, the oil is hot enough to continue.

4. Carefully lower biscuit balls into the oil, cooking no more than a dozen or so at a time.

5. As the doughnuts begin to brown, flip them with tongs.

6. Once browned on both sides, remove doughnuts from the oil and lay on a plate lined with paper towels to drain and cool.

7. Spread confectioners' sugar on a second plate. Roll doughnuts in sugar then serve.

REQUIRED EQUIPMENT:

12-inch camp Dutch oven

Scotty Kimbrell, Fultondale, Alabama
Assistant Scoutmaster
Troop 413, Greater Alabama Council

Servings: 8–10
Preparation Time: ¾ hour
Challenge Level: Moderate

Potawatomi Sticky Bun Bits

"This has been a featured recipe in all of our adult training courses for the past several years. The only problem with this dish is that there is never enough, no matter how much we make."

2 (12-ounce) containers refrigerated biscuit dough

1 cup (2 standard sticks) butter

2 cups dark brown sugar

1 cup chopped pecans

PREPARATION AT CAMP:

1. Remove dough from biscuit containers. Divide each biscuit into pie slice-shaped quarters.

2. Once coals are ready, warm Dutch oven for a few minutes over 25 briquettes.

3. Melt butter in Dutch oven then stir in brown sugar until blended, forming a caramel sauce.

4. Add chopped pecans, mixing and coating with the caramel.

5. Stir dough bits into caramel until all pieces are coated with the sauce.

6. Bake for 35 to 45 minutes using 17 coals on the lid and 8 briquettes under the oven, until biscuits are light golden brown. Refresh coals as required.

REQUIRED EQUIPMENT:

12-inch camp Dutch oven

Robert Harrold, Jefferson, Wisconsin
Executive Board Member
Potawatomi Area Council

Servings: 8–10
Preparation Time: 1¼ hours
Challenge Level: Easy

Darn Good Kielbasa

"For a little color, I like to combine green, red, and yellow bell peppers in this recipe."

2 large onions, cut into ¾-inch-wide strips

3 large bell peppers, cut into ¾-inch-wide strips

2 tablespoons vegetable oil

2 pounds Kielbasa sausage, cut into 1-inch slices

1 (16-ounce) can pineapple chunks in juice (do not drain)

PREPARATION AT CAMP:

1. Preheat Dutch oven over 23 coals.

2. Sauté onions and bell peppers in oil until onions become translucent.

3. Add Kielbasa and pineapple (including the juice).

4. Place lid on oven and cook for about 35 minutes with 16 coals on the lid and 7 briquettes underneath. Refresh coals if required.

REQUIRED EQUIPMENT:

12-inch camp Dutch oven

James Landis, New Providence, Pennsylvania
Unit Commissioner
Conestoga River District, Pennsylvania Dutch Council

Servings: 8–10
Preparation Time: 1¼ hours
Challenge Level: Easy

Preparing breakfast before sunrise. SCOTT H. SIMERLY SR.

Dutch Oven Cinnamon French Toast

PREPARATION AT CAMP:

1. Evenly lay butter slices in bottom of Dutch oven.

2. In a large bowl, combine eggs, half-and-half, brown sugar, vanilla, and cinnamon. Mix well.

3. Dip each slice of bread into egg mixture and arrange the dipped slices in layers in the oven.

4. Pour any remaining egg mixture over the bread in the oven.

5. Bake for 40 to 50 minutes, using 21 coals on the lid and 11 briquettes under the oven, until the bread begins to turn a golden brown. Refresh coals as required.

6. Remove from coals, sprinkle with optional confectioners' sugar or maple syrup, then serve.

REQUIRED EQUIPMENT:
14-inch camp Dutch oven
Large mixing bowl

Delano LaGow, Oswego, Illinois
Committee Member
Troop 31, Three Fires Council

6 tablespoons (¾ standard stick) butter, cut into thin slices

12 eggs

2 cups half-and-half

2 tablespoons brown sugar

2 teaspoons vanilla extract

¼ teaspoon ground cinnamon

1 (1-pound) loaf cinnamon bread or cinnamon raisin bread, sliced

Confectioners' sugar, maple syrup (optional)

Servings: 8–10
Preparation Time: 1¼ hours
Challenge Level: Easy

Flaming Arrow Cheesy Hash Brown Casserole

1 (30-ounce) bag frozen shredded hash brown potatoes, thawed

6 ounces (1½ cups) grated cheddar cheese

1 (10¾-ounce) can condensed cream of chicken soup

1 (10¾-ounce) can condensed cream of celery soup

1 small onion, chopped

½ cup sour cream

2 tablespoons butter, melted

Dash of paprika

PREPARATION AT CAMP:

1. In a large mixing bowl, thoroughly blend together hash brown potatoes, about two-thirds of the grated cheddar cheese, both cans of soup, onion, sour cream, and melted butter.

2. Pour potato mixture into Dutch oven.

3. Bake for about 1 hour, using 14 coals on the lid and 7 briquettes under the oven, until the mixture is bubbly. Refresh coals as required.

4. Remove lid and sprinkle with remaining cheddar cheese along with a dash of paprika.

5. Replace lid and bake for an additional 5 minutes or until cheese is melted.

REQUIRED EQUIPMENT:
10-inch camp Dutch oven
Large mixing bowl

Barry Moore, Tampa, Florida
Former District Chairman
Lake Region District, Gulf Ridge Council

Servings: 8–10
Preparation Time: 1½ hours
Challenge Level: Easy

Three Fires Maple Cream Cheese French Toast

PREPARATION AT CAMP:

1. In a large mixing bowl, blend together the eggs, milk, and 1 cup maple syrup.

2. Arrange half of the bread cubes on the bottom of Dutch oven.

3. Evenly pour about one-third of the egg mixture over the bread cubes.

4. Layer the cubes of cream cheese over the bread.

5. Place the remaining half of the bread cubes over the cheese.

6. Pour the remaining egg mixture over the bread.

7. Using 21 coals on the lid and 11 briquettes under the oven, bake for 45 minutes, refreshing coals as required.

8. Serve with maple syrup to taste.

REQUIRED EQUIPMENT:

14-inch camp Dutch oven
Large mixing bowl

Delano LaGow, Oswego, Illinois
Committee Member
Troop 31, Three Fires Council

1 dozen eggs

1½ cups milk

1 cup maple syrup plus extra for topping

1 loaf French bread, coarsely cubed

2 (8-ounce) packages cream cheese, cubed

Servings: 10–12
Preparation Time: 1 hour
Challenge Level: Easy

Rock Hill Tater Tot Casserole

2 pounds lean ground beef

1 medium onion, chopped

2 cloves garlic, minced

8 ounces sliced fresh mushrooms

1 small jalapeño pepper, chopped

2 (10¾-ounce) cans condensed cream of mushroom soup

1 (2-pound) package frozen Tater Tots, thawed

8 ounces (2 cups) shredded cheddar cheese

Salt and ground black pepper to taste

PREPARATION AT CAMP:

1. Preheat Dutch oven over 25 coals.

2. Brown ground beef, onions, garlic, and mushrooms in the preheated Dutch oven.

3. Transfer browned meat and vegetables to a large bowl.

4. Add jalapeños and cream of mushroom soup to meat and vegetable mixture in the bowl then stir to blend.

5. In the Dutch oven, layer half of the meat and vegetable mixture topped by half of the thawed Tater Tots then topped by half of the shredded cheese.

6. Repeat layers, using the remainder of the ingredients.

7. Bake for 30 to 40 minutes using 17 coals on the lid and 8 briquettes under the oven, until the cheese has melted and the Tater Tots begin to brown. Refresh coals as required.

8. Serve with salt and black pepper to taste.

REQUIRED EQUIPMENT:

12-inch camp Dutch oven
Large mixing bowl

Martha Charles, Rock Hill, South Carolina
Committee Member
Pack 161, Palmetto Council

Craig Charles, Rock Hill, South Carolina
Webelos II Leader
Pack 161, Palmetto Council

Servings: 10–12
Preparation Time: 1¼ hours
Challenge Level: Easy

Big Timber Breakfast Casserole

PREPARATION AT CAMP:

1. Preheat Dutch oven over 25 coals.

2. While oven is warming, mix eggs, powdered mustard, and milk in a large bowl.

3. Brown sausage.

4. Mix bread and apples with the sausage in the oven.

5. Pour egg mixture over bread and sausage.

6. Cover all with cheese.

7. Bake for 30 to 40 minutes, using 17 coals on the lid and 8 briquettes under the oven, until the eggs set. Refresh coals as required.

8. Serve with syrup.

REQUIRED EQUIPMENT:

12-inch camp Dutch oven
Large mixing bowl

Delano LaGow, Oswego, Illinois
Committee Member
Troop 31, Three Fires Council

1 dozen eggs

½ teaspoon powdered mustard

1 cup milk

1 pound Bob Evans Savory Sage pork sausage

1 (1-pound) bread loaf, broken into small pieces

3 Granny Smith apples, peeled, cored, and cut into small pieces

4 ounces (1 cup) shredded cheese

1 (12-ounce) bottle maple syrup

Servings: 10–12
Preparation Time: 1¼ hours
Challenge Level: Easy

Pioneer Pork Chops and Hash Browns

2 pounds boneless pork chops

2 tablespoons vegetable oil

1 (30-ounce) bag frozen shredded hash brown potatoes, thawed

1 (26-ounce) can condensed cream of mushroom soup

1 pound (4 cups) shredded cheese

8 ounces sour cream

1 (2.8-ounce) can French fried onions

PREPARATION AT CAMP:

1. Preheat Dutch oven over 25 coals.

2. Brown the chops in oil on both sides. The pork does not need to be thoroughly cooked on this step. Remove meat and set aside.

3. Combine potatoes, soup, cheese, and sour cream in the oven. Mix well and top with French fried onions.

4. Place the chops over the onions.

5. Bake for about an hour, using 17 coals on the lid and 8 briquettes under the oven, until the chops are cooked through. Refresh coals as needed.

REQUIRED EQUIPMENT:

12-inch camp Dutch oven

Anthony Sullivan, Indianapolis, Indiana
Order of the Arrow and Committee Member
Troop 152, Crossroads of America Council

Servings: 14–16
Preparation Time: 1¾ hours
Challenge Level: Easy

Zoom Flume 'Shrooms

"Zoom Flume is a Class III rapid on the Arkansas River near BSA's Rocky Mountain High Adventure Base in Colorado. Zoom Flume is just upstream of Toilet Bowl Rapid and just downstream of Hemorrhoid Rock. Our troop has made regular trips to Rocky Mountain Base, and the highlight each year is shooting the rapids on the Arkansas. This recipe, named in honor of the Zoom, is an easy and flexible dish that can also be cooked in foil over an open fire or camp stove if a Dutch oven is not available."

4 slices bacon

4 portobello mushroom caps

1 tomato

2 cloves garlic, diced

8 ounces (2 cups) shredded mozzarella cheese

Salt and ground black pepper to taste

Option: For a vegetarian version, delete the bacon and lightly cover the bottom of the Dutch oven with vegetable oil before preheating to prevent the mushroom caps from sticking.

PREPARATION AT CAMP:

1. Preheat Dutch oven over 23 coals.

2. Fry bacon until crispy in preheated Dutch oven. Set bacon aside. Do not drain grease from the oven.

3. While bacon is cooking, wash mushrooms and cut tomato into four slices, each no more than about ¼ inch thick.

4. Fill the inside of each mushroom cap with diced garlic and about half of the shredded cheese, divided evenly between each mushroom.

5. Crumble crispy bacon over the cheese and garlic.

6. Place a tomato slice over the cheese on each mushroom. Sprinkle salt and black pepper to taste over the tomato slices.

7. Spread the mushroom caps in the bottom of the preheated Dutch oven and cook for about 15 minutes, using 7 coals under the oven and 16 briquettes on the lid.

8. Remove the lid and cover the mushroom caps with the remainder of the shredded cheese. Replace lid and allow cheese to melt for a couple of minutes before serving.

REQUIRED EQUIPMENT:

12-inch camp Dutch oven

David Visser, Hurst, Texas
Assistant Scoutmaster
Troop 340, Longhorn Council

Servings: 4
Preparation Time: 1 hour
Challenge Level: Easy

2 (8-ounce) containers refrigerated crescent roll dough

1 (5-ounce) pouch Boboli Original pizza sauce

4 ounces (1 cup) shredded mozzarella cheese

3 ounces chopped pepperoni

No-Fuss Pizza Roll-ups

"This recipe is great for new Scouts who are just learning how to cook, or for a quick meal after a long day of adventure. It's always a crowd pleaser with a hungry troop."

PREPARATION AT CAMP:

1. Preheat Dutch oven using 18 coals on the lid and 9 briquettes under the oven.

2. Unroll crescent dough from containers.

3. Divide pizza sauce, cheese, and pepperoni among the crescents and roll up each like a jellyroll.

4. Bake for 15 to 20 minutes, until the crescent rolls become a golden brown.

REQUIRED EQUIPMENT:

12-inch camp Dutch oven

Craig Depuy, Clemmons, North Carolina
Assistant Scoutmaster and Troop Chaplain
Troop 731, Old Hickory Council

Servings: 4–6
Preparation Time: ¾ hour
Challenge Level: Easy

Slicing taters in the Mojave Desert.
SCOTT H. SIMERLY SR.

Wrappin' Micro Potstickers

"I was the young cook on an outing and needed to prepare fried food but didn't have a skillet. I told my dad of the dilemma, and, with a wry grin, he said, 'Sure you have a skillet. You just have to know where to look.' He then proceeded to remove the lid from his Dutch oven, flip it over, and put it on the coals. At my expression of shock, he said, 'It's often not about the tools and ingredients you want or need; it's about using what you have.' And that is when I learned to think and cook outside the proverbial box.

"This is a modification of a dessert recipe of mine. Asian wrappers are extremely versatile and fun to experiment with because almost any filling works."

½ (12-ounce / 50-count) package medium-size wonton or gyoza wrappers

1½ cups tuna, diced ham, or diced salami (or ½ cup each)

¾ cup finely chopped onion, cabbage, or carrots (or ¼ cup each)

½ cup grated hard cheese, your choice

½ cup olive oil

Canola oil for frying

PREPARATION AT CAMP:

1. Flip the lid of the Dutch oven and support it on rocks or other heat-proof stand an inch or so over about 25 coals to warm the lid.

2. Place several wrappers on a flat surface and spoon about a tablespoon of meat onto half of each wrapper.

3. Sprinkle vegetables and cheese over meat filling.

4. Dampen edge of wrapper and fold in half, sealing edge with a fork or fingers. Do not overfill the wrappers.

5. Brush each wrapper with olive oil.

6. Fry the potstickers until browned on each side.

REQUIRED EQUIPMENT:

12-inch camp Dutch oven

Curt "The Titanium Chef" White, Forks, Washington
Committee Member
Troop 1467, Chief Seattle Council

TIPS:
- Dipping sauces are fun to have with this recipe.
- Flipped over, the concave inside surface of a Dutch oven lid makes for a great substitute "wok." With coals concentrated to the center under the lid, the main frying can proceed from the hot center outward to the cooler perimeter.
- To double the cooking capacity and cut the total cooking time, the base of the Dutch oven can be used as a frying pan along with the lid.

Servings: 4–6
Preparation Time: ¾ hour
Challenge Level: Moderate

Schoellkopf Buffalo Pizza

1 (11-ounce) container refrigerated Pillsbury Thin Pizza Crust

1 pound frozen breaded chicken fingers

½ cup (1 standard stick) butter, melted

4 tablespoons hot sauce

½ cup blue cheese salad dressing

⅓ cup grated provolone cheese

Option: Double the hot sauce for real Buffalo heat.

"This recipe is named for our local council camp, the place where I created this treat. I always try to prepare a Dutch oven goodie at each troop campout. We love our hot wings here in Buffalo, so this was a natural for us."

PREPARATION AT CAMP:

1. Line Dutch oven with aluminum foil then grease the foil.

2. Unroll pizza dough into the oven. Fold the edges of the dough under to fully fit inside the oven and to create a thicker edge to the crust.

3. Chop chicken fingers into bite-size pieces.

4. In a medium-size mixing bowl, combine melted butter with the hot sauce.

5. Add chicken pieces to the sauce mixture and thoroughly coat.

6. Pour coated chicken and sauce into oven and spread evenly over the dough.

7. Pour blue cheese dressing over chicken pieces and cover all with provolone cheese.

8. Bake for 30 minutes using 19 coals on the lid and 10 briquettes under the oven, until bottom of crust is brown and cheese is melted.

REQUIRED EQUIPMENT:
12-inch camp Dutch oven
Medium-size mixing bowl
Heavy-duty aluminum foil

Rick Pickelhaupt, Amherst, New York
Eagle Scout and Scoutmaster
Troop 457, Greater Niagara Frontier Council

Servings: 4–6
Preparation Time: 1 hour
Challenge Level: Easy

Chicken Bake Thingy

"The name of the dish comes from Wood Badge. Everything at Wood Badge is called a 'Thingy.' I was a staffer on the course and volunteered to help with the cooking demonstration at Camp Davy Crockett, but I didn't have a name for my recipe. As the candidates walked through the various cooking stations, they would sample the dishes. Later, one of the patrols told me that they really liked the 'Chicken Bake Thingy.'"

2 (8-ounce) containers garlic butter-flavored Pillsbury Crescent rolls

2 (9¾-ounce) cans white chunk chicken, drained

1 (16-ounce) container sour cream

1 teaspoon celery salt

1 tablespoon cornmeal

¼ cup shredded Parmesan cheese

PREPARATION AT CAMP:

1. Unroll crescent dough from one container and spread evenly across the bottom of greased Dutch oven.

2. Mix chicken, sour cream, and celery salt in a medium-size bowl.

3. Using 16 coals on the lid and 7 briquettes under the oven, bake crescent dough for 10 minutes.

4. Remove Dutch oven from coals and spread chicken mixture over baked dough.

5. Unroll dough from second container and spread evenly over chicken mixture.

6. Sprinkle cornmeal and Parmesan cheese over dough.

7. Return Dutch oven to coals and continue to bake until top of dough becomes a light brown, about 30 additional minutes.

TIP: Keep crescent roll containers chilled until time to use because dough that has become warm is sticky and difficult to unroll.

REQUIRED EQUIPMENT:

12-inch camp Dutch oven
Medium-size mixing bowl

Joe Yates, Lebanon, Virginia
Scoutmaster
Troop 408, Sequoyah Council

Servings: 6–8
Preparation Time: 1 hour
Challenge Level: Easy

63

½ cup sour cream

1 (16-ounce) can chili beans, drained

1 (11-ounce) can mexicorn, drained

1 (16-ounce) jar mild chunky salsa

4 green bell peppers, halved and seeded

1 cup Mexican blend shredded cheese

Kicked-Up Peppers

"This recipe was developed to challenge young Scouts to prepare things besides hot dogs and PBJ sandwiches. By learning to cook simple, tasty meals in a Dutch oven, they become used to this style of cooking and develop more confidence, trying dishes that require a little more skill. They eventually become proficient at putting together good meals all by themselves."

PREPARATION AT CAMP:

1. Preheat Dutch oven using 7 coals under the oven and 16 briquettes on the lid.

2. Combine sour cream, chili beans, mexicorn, and salsa in a medium-size bowl.

3. Divide the bean mix evenly among the peppers, filling each pepper half.

4. Lay filled peppers in preheated Dutch oven and bake for about 45 minutes.

5. Remove peppers from oven and garnish with shredded cheese.

REQUIRED EQUIPMENT:

12-inch camp Dutch oven
Medium-size mixing bowl

James Landis, New Providence, Pennsylvania
Unit Commissioner
Conestoga River District, Pennsylvania Dutch Council

Servings: 8
Preparation Time: 1 hour
Challenge Level: Easy

Ozark Chicken Alfredo Potpie

"As Scoutmasters, we try to inspire the boys to cook more than hot dogs in their Patrols. We cook good meals for ourselves so the boys can observe that it can be done and that it doesn't have to take a lot of work."

PREPARATION AT CAMP:

1. Line bottom of Dutch oven with one package of crescent roll dough.

2. Spread Alfredo sauce over dough.

3. Add chunk chicken, salt and black pepper, canned vegetables, and cheese over Alfredo sauce.

4. Use dough from second crescent roll package to form top crust.

5. Bake for about 30 minutes using 17 coals on the lid and 8 briquettes under the oven, until the top turns a golden brown.

REQUIRED EQUIPMENT:

12-inch camp Dutch oven

Brad Hanson, Crane, Missouri
Assistant Scoutmaster
Troop 372, Ozark Trails Council

2 (8-ounce) containers refrigerated crescent roll dough

1 (15-ounce) jar Alfredo sauce

2 (12½-ounce) cans chunk chicken, drained

Salt and ground black pepper to taste

1 (15-ounce) can vegetable blend (peas, carrots, etc.), drained

8 ounces (2 cups) shredded mozzarella cheese

A lot of chopping calls for teamwork! SCOTT H.

SIMERLY SR.

Servings: 8–10
Preparation Time: ¾ hour
Challenge Level: Easy

Father and Son's Venison Chili

2 pounds ground venison

1 large onion, chopped

2 (15-ounce) cans chili with beans

2 (15-ounce) cans baked beans

8 ounces (2 cups) sharp shredded cheese

Hot sauce (optional)

Option: Goes great with Fritos corn chips.

"Hunting is a great father-son sport that seems to be overlooked anymore. To me, it goes right along with Scouting. What could be better than going hunting with your father, bagging a deer, then cooking it later at Scout camp? That is something to remember for the rest of your life. I used this recipe at our last campout, and Scouts and den leaders were begging for a bowl. I knew it was a hit when one leader came by and said, 'Well, since my Scouts are eating your chili instead of mine, I guess it must be good.'"

PREPARATION AT CAMP:

1. Preheat Dutch oven for a few minutes over 20 coals.

2. Brown the venison along with the onion in preheated Dutch oven.

3. Add the chili with beans and baked beans. Stir then simmer for 30 minutes.

4. Top with cheese. Serve with optional hot sauce.

REQUIRED EQUIPMENT:

12-inch camp Dutch oven

David Burch, Springfield, Ohio
Former Den Leader
Pack 313, Tecumseh Council

Servings: 8–10
Preparation Time: 1 hour
Challenge Level: Easy

Cub-O-Ree Mexican Lasagna

"We first used this recipe at a Cub-O-Ree that had an Olympic theme. Each Pack was to represent a country. Our Pack chose to represent Mexico. The boys cooked Mexican Lasagna and entered it into the entree division for the Dutch oven cook-off. They won first place! The same group of boys moved up to Boy Scouts together and still use this recipe on camping trips. They love it."

PREPARATION AT CAMP:

1. Brown the ground beef in a medium-size frying pan.

2. Add salsa, tomato sauce, and refried beans to the beef then simmer on low heat for about 10 minutes.

3. Line Dutch oven with aluminum foil.

4. Place 1 tortilla on the bottom of the Dutch oven. Tear a second tortilla in half to fill in the open gaps and create a solid layer of tortillas.

5. Spoon about a third of the beef mixture in a layer on top of tortillas then spread another third of the shredded cheese in a layer over the beef.

6. Add another tortilla, with torn tortilla pieces, then a third of beef mixture and a third of cheese.

7. Repeat once more with remainder of tortillas, beef, and cheese.

8. Heat for about 30 minutes using 16 coals on the lid and 7 briquettes under the oven.

REQUIRED EQUIPMENT:
12-inch camp Dutch oven
Medium-size frying pan
Heavy-duty aluminum foil

April Walker, Wallace, North Carolina
Committee Member
Troop 35, Tuscarora Council

1½ pounds lean ground beef

1 (16-ounce) jar salsa (your favorite)

1 (8-ounce) can tomato sauce

1 (16-ounce) can refried beans

1 (8-count) package 8-inch flour tortillas

8 ounces (2 cups) Mexican blend shredded cheese

Servings: 8–10
Preparation Time: 1 hour
Challenge Level: Moderate

1½ pounds lean
ground beef or turkey

1 small onion, chopped

1 (28-ounce) can
baked beans

1 (18-ounce) bottle
barbecue sauce

2 (12-ounce) containers
refrigerated biscuit dough

8 ounces (2 cups)
grated cheese

Beanie Bake

"A one-pot meal that everyone in the troop enjoys."

PREPARATION AT CAMP:

1. In a Dutch oven over 25 coals, brown the meat with the onions.

2. Add baked beans and barbeque sauce to the cooked meat and onions. Mix well.

3. Distribute biscuits evenly over top of the bean mixture.

4. Bake for about 30 minutes using 17 coals on the lid and 8 briquettes under the oven, until the tops of the biscuits become golden brown.

5. Remove lid and sprinkle grated cheese over the biscuits.

6. Cover with lid for a few additional minutes to allow cheese to melt before serving.

REQUIRED EQUIPMENT:

12-inch camp Dutch oven

Mike Russell, Harker Heights, Texas
Scoutmaster
Troop 229, Longhorn Council

Servings: 10–12
Preparation Time: 1 hour
Challenge Level: Easy

Adirondack Spicy Chicken Tortilla Dip

"This recipe comes from folks up in the Adirondack Mountains of New York. Guaranteed to help keep you warm on a cool night."

PREPARATION AT CAMP:

1. Combine chicken, RedHot sauce, cream cheese, ranch dressing, and cheddar cheese in the Dutch oven. Mix ingredients thoroughly.

2. Bake for about 30 minutes using 17 briquettes on the lid and 8 coals under the oven.

3. Serve with tortilla chips.

REQUIRED EQUIPMENT:

12-inch camp Dutch oven

Craig Depuy, Clemmons, North Carolina
Assistant Scoutmaster and Troop Chaplain
Troop 731, Old Hickory Council

1 (22-ounce) bag Tyson Grilled & Ready chicken breasts, diced

1 cup Frank's RedHot Original Sauce

2 (8-ounce) packages cream cheese, softened

1 cup ranch dressing

8 ounces (2 cups) shredded cheddar cheese

2 (13-ounce) bags tortilla chips

Another great Dutch oven dish gets ready for the coals. SCOTT H. SIMERLY SR.

Servings: 14–16
Preparation Time: ¾ hour
Challenge Level: Easy

Pollo a la Roma

"We had this dish while we vacationed in Rome. The restaurant baked theirs in a brick outdoor oven, but I adapted it to the Dutch oven."

1 (4-pound) whole chicken, gutted and cleaned

1 (14-ounce) can chicken broth

About 2 pounds fresh vegetables, such as celery, leeks, carrots, and potatoes, all chopped into bite-size pieces

¼ teaspoon basil, fresh or dried

¼ teaspoon parsley, fresh or dried

¼ teaspoon rosemary, fresh or dried

Salt and ground black pepper to taste

½ pound pancetta

Option: Regular bacon can be substituted for the pancetta (Italian bacon).

PREPARATION AT CAMP:

1. Place chicken on trivet or rack in the Dutch oven.

2. Pour broth over chicken and place vegetables in the broth surrounding the chicken.

3. Rub the herbs and spices all over the skin then drape the pancetta over the chicken.

4. Cook for about an hour using 21 coals on the lid and 11 briquettes under the oven. Refresh coals as required.

REQUIRED EQUIPMENT:

Deep 14-inch camp Dutch oven with trivet

Beverly Jo Antonini, Morgantown, West Virginia
Assistant Scoutmaster
Troop 49, Mountaineer Area Council

Mmmmm—basil adds flavor and aroma! CHRISTINE CONNERS

Servings: 6–8
Preparation Time: 1¼ hours
Challenge Level: Easy

Camp Crown Teriyaki Chicken

"Camp Crown is the name of a council-owned camp in our area and the first place I served this dish to our troop members. During our annual outing to Camp Crown, the troop prepares a family-style dinner when everyone brings their individually prepared meals to a central table where a few of the adults judge the recipes. When this dish was presented, only a few people took a sample because it didn't look very appetizing. But once one of the boys tried it, the word spread, and it turned out to be the Meal of the Campout."

PREPARATION AT CAMP:

1. Blend ranch dressing, soy sauce, and teriyaki sauce together in a small bowl.

2. Lay chicken breasts on the bottom of the Dutch oven.

3. Pour dressing sauce over chicken.

4. Cover chicken with green onions and bacon bits.

5. Bake for about an hour using 18 coals on the lid and 9 briquettes under the oven, until the chicken is fully cooked.

REQUIRED EQUIPMENT:
12-inch camp Dutch oven
Small mixing bowl

Kevin Wehde, Grayslake, Illinois
Eagle Scout and Assistant Scoutmaster
Troop 96, Northeast Illinois Council

½ cup Hidden Valley Ranch Dressing

¼ cup low-sodium soy sauce

½ cup teriyaki sauce

3 pounds boneless skinless chicken breasts

3 green onions, chopped

1 (3-ounce) package real bacon bits or pieces

Option: This recipe is delicious over rice or potatoes.

Servings: 6–8
Preparation Time: 1¼ hours
Challenge Level: Easy

Portobello Pork Olé

2 cups chopped
portobello mushrooms

8 ounces (2 cups)
shredded cheddar cheese

3 tablespoons maple
syrup

1 (24-ounce) jar mild
Pace picante sauce

2 pounds pork loin,
cut in 1-inch cubes

¼ cup snipped
fresh parsley

"Perhaps in reading this recipe, you'd think that the maple syrup in the ingredients list is a mistake. But *don't* leave it out! It is what makes this dish amazingly good. So good, in fact, that it won first place at the Duchesne County Fair Dutch Oven Contest."

PREPARATION AT CAMP:

1. Combine mushrooms, cheddar cheese, and maple syrup in a medium-size bowl.

2. Pour picante sauce into Dutch oven and arrange pork cubes over sauce.

3. Pour mushroom mix over cubed pork in Dutch oven.

4. Bake for 1 hour using 18 coals on the lid and 9 briquettes under the oven.

5. Remove from heat, sprinkle parsley snips over pork and salsa, then serve.

REQUIRED EQUIPMENT:

12-inch camp Dutch oven
Medium-size bowl

John Foster, Duchesne, Utah
District Commissioner
Kings Peak District, Utah National Parks Council

Servings: 6–8
Preparation Time: 1¼ hours
Challenge Level: Easy

Boy Scout Chicken

"There are two ways to prepare this recipe: 1) place the chicken inside a Dutch oven using a random amount of coals, go play for an hour, come back hungry, then whine because either it didn't fully cook or because it became a crispy critter; or, 2) follow the simple directions below."

PREPARATION AT CAMP:

1. Place chicken in Dutch oven.

2. Cover with barbecue sauce.

3. Bake for about 1¼ hours using 18 coals on the lid and 9 briquettes under the oven. Refresh coals as required.

REQUIRED EQUIPMENT:

12-inch camp Dutch oven

Jim Landis, New Providence, Pennsylvania
Unit Commissioner
Conestoga River District, Pennsylvania Dutch Council

1 whole chicken, about 5 pounds, gutted, washed, and cut up

1 (16-ounce) bottle barbecue sauce

Option: The chicken can also be cooked whole in a deep 12-inch Dutch oven using the same coal count and cooking time.

Servings: 6–8
Preparation Time: 1½ hours
Challenge Level: Easy

MARINADE:

½ cup soy sauce

2 teaspoons fresh ginger, chopped fine

2 pounds flank, round, or sirloin steak, sliced diagonally into thin strips

SAUCE:

¼ cup soy sauce

2 tablespoons cornstarch

1 tablespoon rice vinegar

2 tablespoons brown sugar

½ cup water

1 beef seasoning packet (from ramen noodle package)

2 heads fresh broccoli

1 large onion

3 (3-ounce) packages beef-flavor ramen noodles

¼ cup peanut oil

Options: In place of or in addition to the broccoli, use bok choy, mung bean sprouts, fresh garlic, bell pepper, sliced carrots, fresh shiitake mushrooms, celery, zucchini, sesame seeds, green beans, firm tofu, chicken, or shrimp.

Serves 6–8
Preparation Time: 1½ hours
Challenge level: Difficult

Chinese Beef and Broccoli with Ramen Noodles

"This recipe demonstrates the versatility of a Dutch oven. You can even use it like a wok."

PREPARATION AT CAMP:

1. In a large ziplock bag, prepare marinade by mixing ½ cup soy sauce and ginger.

2. Add steak strips to ziplock bag. Seal the bag and shake to distribute marinade. Place in cooler for at least an hour.

3. While beef marinates, prepare sauce by combining ¼ cup soy sauce, cornstarch, vinegar, brown sugar, water, and seasoning packet in a small bowl.

4. Cut broccoli into florets, chop optional vegetables into pieces of consistent size, and slice onion into wedges.

5. Cook ramen noodles in a small pot. Drain noodles and set aside. Do not use the noodle seasoning packets here.

6. Heat oil in well-seasoned Dutch oven over 45 coals until hot.

7. Stir-fry the marinated beef in peanut oil until browned. Discard marinade.

8. Add broccoli, onion, and sauce then stir-fry for an additional 3 to 5 minutes, cooking until the vegetables are crisp-tender and the sauce thickens.

9. Add cooked ramen noodles and stir.

10. Remove from heat and serve.

REQUIRED EQUIPMENT:

16-inch camp Dutch oven
Small cook pot
Small mixing bowl
Large ziplock bag (at least 1-gallon size)

David Anderson, Meadville, Pennsylvania
Scoutmaster
Troop 244, French Creek Council

Trial-by-Fire Barbecue Ribs

"This recipe had fewer ingredients until one outing when I had remembered to bring along my Dutch oven but realized I had forgotten to pack the store-bought barbecue sauce. One of the Scouts had a can of warm Dr Pepper, and that was the beginning of this sauce. Other ingredients were scrounged from other campers on that fateful evening. What you see below is the best of several trials by the fire."

PREPARATION AT CAMP:

1. Add all ingredients except ribs to a medium-size cook pot and stir well.

2. Bring the sauce to a slow boil over medium flame. Reduce heat and simmer for 10 minutes. Remove pot from the flame and set aside.

3. Preheat Dutch oven over 25 coals.

4. Brown the meat in preheated Dutch oven. The meat does not need to be thoroughly cooked in this step.

5. Pour sauce over the meat in the Dutch oven.

6. Cook for 1½ hours using 15 coals on the lid and 10 briquettes under the oven. Refresh coals as required. When the ribs are ready to serve, they will be fallin' off the bone.

REQUIRED EQUIPMENT:

12-inch camp Dutch oven
Medium-size cook pot

Brett Morehead, Ardmore, Oklahoma
Scoutmaster
Troop 5, Arbuckle Area Council

1 cup Dr Pepper

2 cups Heinz ketchup

¼ cup Lea & Perrins Worcestershire sauce

¼ cup A1 Steak Sauce

¼ cup brown sugar

2 teaspoons ground black pepper

1 teaspoon garlic powder

1 teaspoon dried onion flakes

1 teaspoon liquid smoke

6–8 country-style pork ribs

Options: Several other types of meat work well here, including bone-in or bone-out pork chops, and short ribs.

Servings: 6–8
Preparation Time: 2 hours
Challenge Level: Moderate

Bobwhite Cornish Hen Stew

4 Cornish hens, thawed

32 ounces chicken stock

1 (14½-ounce) can Italian diced tomatoes (with basil, garlic, and oregano)

1 (2-pound) package frozen vegetables for stew (potatoes, carrots, onions, celery)

2 (7-ounce) cans sliced mushrooms, drained

1 (0.87-ounce) envelope McCormick's Grill Mates Tomato, Garlic, and Basil Marinade mix

"When I went to Wood Badge, I was assigned to the Bobwhite Patrol; and for two weekends, all the Bobwhites talked about was what they were going to eat. So at Ransburg Scout Camp, I entered a Dutch oven cook-off for the leaders with the newly created Bobwhite Stew. It won first place!"

PREPARATION AT CAMP:

1. Put hens, stock, tomatoes, vegetables, and mushrooms into Dutch oven.

2. Sprinkle hens with marinade mix.

3. Bake for about 1 hour using 17 coals on the lid and 8 briquettes under the oven, until the meat is fully cooked.

REQUIRED EQUIPMENT:

12-inch camp Dutch oven

William Hofheins, Franklin, Indiana
Eagle Scout and Committee Member
Troop 256, Crossroads of America Council

TIPS: If chicken stock is unavailable, broth can be substituted. Divide hens in half by cutting along the backbone after baking.

Servings: 8 (2 servings per hen)
Preparation Time: 1¼ hours
Challenge Level: Easy

Erie Shores Cabbage Rolls

PREPARATION AT CAMP:

1. Mix ground beef, sausage, rice, pizza sauce, onion, bell pepper, and chopped pepperoni together in a large mixing bowl.

2. Form 8 fist-size meatballs, and wrap each meatball with one cabbage leaf.

3. Place each meatball with the cabbage seam-side down in Dutch oven.

4. Cover cabbage rolls with green beans and stewed tomatoes.

5. Bake for 75 minutes using 17 coals on the lid and 8 briquettes under the oven, until meat is fully cooked. Refresh coals as required.

REQUIRED EQUIPMENT:

12-inch camp Dutch oven
Large mixing bowl

John Bailey, Bowling Green, Ohio
Assistant Scoutmaster
Troop 337, Erie Shores Council

1 pound lean ground beef

1 pound ground sausage

¾ cup instant rice

10 ounces pizza sauce

1 medium onion, chopped

1 green bell pepper, chopped

1¼ inch stack pepperoni slices, chopped

8 cabbage leaves

1 (14½-ounce) can French-cut green beans, drained

1 (14½-ounce) can stewed tomatoes

Servings: 8
Preparation Time: 1¾ hours
Challenge Level: Easy

Boy Scout Potato Boats

8 medium baking
potatoes, scrubbed,
baked, and cooled

1 pound ground sausage

8 eggs

1 teaspoon seasoned salt

½ teaspoon ground black
pepper

2 cups grated cheese

1 (16-ounce) jar salsa
(optional)

Option: This recipe also
makes a fine breakfast,
particularly if the potatoes
are baked the night before.
This reduces the preparation
time to about an hour.

TIP: There are
numerous ways to bake
potatoes. Here's an easy
one: Wrap each in heavy
foil and bury in the coals of
the campfire for a half hour
to an hour. Occasionally
rotate.

PREPARATION AT CAMP:

1. Slice off the top ¼–½ inch from the length of each baked potato.

2. Cut the flesh (i.e., the "insides") of each potato into a checkerboard pattern. Scoop out the flesh and set aside.

3. In Dutch oven over 23 coals, brown the sausage then add the reserved potato flesh. Brown the potato flesh with the sausage. Remove oven from the coals.

4. Divide the sausage and potato mixture among the eight potato skin "boats."

5. Whisk the eggs in a medium-size bowl. Blend in the seasoned salt and black pepper.

6. Pour some of the egg mixture into the boats until each is filled. (Any remaining potato and egg mixture can be cooked separately in a foil package in the campfire, if desired.)

7. Top each boat with grated cheese.

8. Set the potato boats into the still-warm Dutch oven. Using 15 coals on the lid and 8 briquettes under the oven, cook for about 30 minutes, until the eggs become firm. Refresh coals as required.

9. Remove potato boats from the oven and top with optional salsa, if desired.

REQUIRED EQUIPMENT:
12-inch camp Dutch oven
Medium-size mixing bowl

Ken Vetrovec, Racine, Wisconsin
Eagle Scout and Woodbadge Coordinator
Troop 634, Southeast Wisconsin Council

Servings: 8
Preparation Time: 2 hours
Challenge Level: Moderate

Crew 60 Easy Enchiladas

"Crew 60 is a Native American/Order of the Arrow dance team, and our crew's enchilada recipe won first place at the local Scout-o-Rama!"

PREPARATION AT CAMP:

1. Pour in and spread enough enchilada sauce to cover bottom of Dutch oven.

2. Stack taquitos over enchilada sauce in oven.

3. Pour remaining enchilada sauce over taquitos.

4. Bake for 30 to 40 minutes using 17 coals on the lid and 8 briquettes under the oven, until the sauce is bubbling.

5. Top with diced peppers and onions then sprinkle cheese over the top.

6. Cover and set for about 5 more minutes, until the cheese is fully melted.

REQUIRED EQUIPMENT:

12-inch camp Dutch oven

David and Janet Stanger, Boise, Idaho
Committee Members
Crew 60, Ore-Ida Council

2 (16-ounce) cans enchilada sauce

1 box (about 25) frozen taquitos, thawed

1 small green bell pepper, diced

1 small red bell pepper, diced

1 small yellow bell pepper, diced

6–8 green onions, diced

1 pound (4 cups) shredded Mexican-blend cheese

Servings: 8–10
Preparation Time: 1¼ hours
Challenge Level: Easy

Big Sky Jambalaya

1 pound boneless chicken, cut into small pieces

¼ cup (½ standard stick) butter

1 pound Kielbasa sausage, sliced into ½-inch pieces

1 medium green pepper, diced

1 medium onion, diced

2 stalks celery, diced

2 (10-ounce) cans Ro*Tel tomatoes, diced

1 (14½-ounce) can chicken broth

½ pound shrimp, peeled

2 cups instant rice

¼ teaspoon salt

PREPARATION AT CAMP:

1. Preheat Dutch oven over 25 coals.

2. Cook chicken in melted butter until no trace of pink remains.

3. Add sausage, green pepper, onion, and celery. Cook until vegetables are just tender.

4. Mix in tomatoes and chicken broth. Bring to a full boil, refreshing coals as needed.

5. Add shrimp and cook an additional 5 minutes.

6. Stir in rice and salt.

7. Cover. Remove from heat. Let stand 5 minutes. Fluff with a fork.

REQUIRED EQUIPMENT:

12-inch camp Dutch oven

Robert Dowdy, Great Falls, Montana
Venturing Roundtable Commissioner
Crew 2001, Montana Council

Servings: 8–10
Preparation Time: 1¼ hours
Challenge Level: Easy

Southwestern Chili

PREPARATION AT CAMP:

1. Preheat Dutch oven over 25 coals.

2. Sauté the onions and garlic in oil until the onions become translucent.

3. Add ground turkey or beef and brown the meat until no longer pink.

4. Add remaining items, except for pasta, and cook for about 30 minutes, covered, with no briquettes on the lid. Refresh coals if required. If simmer becomes too vigorous, remove some of the coals from under the oven.

5. Add pasta to oven and cook for an additional 10 minutes.

REQUIRED EQUIPMENT:

12-inch camp Dutch oven

Donald Voss, Marysville, Ohio
Webelos Den Leader
Troop 101, Simon Kenton Council

1 small onion, diced

3 cloves garlic, minced

2 tablespoons cooking oil

1 pound lean ground beef or ground turkey

1 (15-ounce) can sweet corn, drained

1 (15-ounce) can black beans (do not drain)

1 (14-ounce) can chicken broth

1 (24-ounce) jar salsa

1 cup uncooked small shell pasta

Servings: 8–10
Preparation Time: 1½ hours
Challenge Level: Easy

1½ pounds ground beef

¾ cup Bisquick baking mix

12 saltine crackers, crushed

½ cup chopped onion

½ cup chopped green pepper

2 tablespoons ketchup

⅛ teaspoon ground black pepper

1 (14-ounce) can beef broth, divided

3 medium potatoes, peeled and cut into wedges

1 pound fresh green beans, stemmed

5 slices processed American cheese

1 (4-ounce) can sliced mushrooms, drained

Options: The onions, green pepper, and mushrooms can be considered optional depending on tastes; thinly sliced carrots can be substituted for the green beans.

Patrol Meat Loaf

"This is a great recipe for a Patrol. We field-tested it at an annual fall Camporee, at the time when the potatoes are freshly harvested here in Aroostook County, Maine. Delicious! This recipe won a Grand Prize ribbon at the Northern Maine Fair in 2010."

PREPARATION AT CAMP:

1. In a medium-size mixing bowl, combine ground beef, baking mix, crushed saltines, onion, green pepper, ketchup, black pepper, and ¼ cup of the beef broth.

2. Pat meat loaf flat on the bottom of Dutch oven, leaving a 1-inch gap between the loaf and the wall of the oven around the perimeter.

3. Place potato wedges on top of meat loaf in a spoke-like fashion.

4. Place green beans on top of the potatoes.

5. Pour remaining broth in the moat around the edge of the meat loaf.

6. Cover and bake for about an hour using 18 coals on the lid and 9 briquettes under the oven, until the meat is fully cooked and the potatoes are tender. Refresh coals as required.

7. Remove oven from coals then layer the cheese over the green beans.

8. Sprinkle drained mushrooms over the cheese.

9. Replace cover and allow to rest until the cheese melts, about 5 to 10 minutes.

REQUIRED EQUIPMENT:
12-inch camp Dutch oven
Medium-size mixing bowl

Kathryn Peary, Presque Isle, Maine
Committee Chairman
Pack 171, Katahdin Area Council

Servings: 8–10
Preparation Time: 1½ hours
Challenge Level: Easy

Chicken Dutchiladas

"This recipe was awarded second place in the entree category in *Scouting* magazine's 2009 Great Tastes in Camp Cooking contest."

PREPARATION AT CAMP:

1. Boil boneless chicken pieces in a medium-size pot until thoroughly heated. Slice and pull cooked meat to produce about 3 cups shredded chicken.

2. Preheat Dutch oven over 25 coals.

3. In the preheated Dutch oven, lightly fry both sides of each tortilla in a small amount of oil until crisp. Drain oil from fried tortillas by layering between paper towels. Set tortillas aside and remove oven from coals for the moment.

4. In a large bowl, add cooked chicken, sour cream, dry ranch dressing mix, olives, about a third of the green enchilada sauce, and about a third of the shredded cheese. Mix well.

5. Carefully line the hot Dutch oven with heavy-duty aluminum foil and wet the foil at bottom with a little of the remaining green enchilada sauce.

6. Distribute three tortillas over green sauce at bottom of oven, followed by about a third of the chicken mixture, about a quarter of the remaining shredded cheese, and about a quarter of the remaining green enchilada sauce.

7. Add a second layer, spreading three more tortillas over the top of the first layer. Follow with some of the remaining chicken mixture, shredded cheese, and green enchilada sauce. Repeat once again to produce a third layer.

8. At this point, three tortillas and only a small amount of shredded cheese and green enchilada sauce should remain. Arrange the three tortillas across the top and spread the remaining enchilada sauce and shredded cheese over all.

9. Cover Dutch oven and cook for 30 minutes using 18 coals on the lid and 7 briquettes under the oven. Refresh coals if necessary.

Ellen Bergman,
Whittier, California
Committee Chair
Pack 673, Los Angeles Area Council

1½ pounds boneless chicken pieces, enough to produce about 3 cups shredded meat

12 (6-inch) corn tortillas

Small amount of vegetable oil for frying tortillas

1 (16-ounce) container sour cream

1 (1-ounce) package dry ranch dressing mix

½ cup sliced black olives

1 (10-ounce) can green enchilada sauce

12 ounces (3 cups) shredded Monterey Jack or cheddar cheese

REQUIRED EQUIPMENT:
12-inch camp Dutch oven
Medium-size cook pot
Large mixing bowl
Heavy-duty aluminum foil

Servings: 8–10
Preparation Time: 1½ hours
Challenge Level: Moderate

Wild Outdoors Meat Loaf

2 pounds ground venison

1½ pounds ground chuck

1 sleeve (about 4 ounces) Ritz crackers, crumbled

2 (1.1-ounce) packages Lipton Beefy Onion soup mix

¼ cup ketchup

¼ cup Heinz 57 sauce

2 tablespoons Worcestershire sauce

1 egg

"I get tired of the same old spaghetti and chili dinners. I tell my Scouts that, with a little more work, time, and ingredients, they can have a gourmet meal. Here is one of them."

PREPARATION AT CAMP:

1. In a large bowl, mix venison and chuck together.

2. Add crackers and soup mix to the ground meat then blend.

3. Add ketchup, sauces, and egg to the meat mix and thoroughly combine.

4. Separate meat mixture into two equal amounts and form each into a loaf of even depth and of a size such that both will fit side by side in a 9-inch pie pan.

5. Preheat Dutch oven with 18 coals on the lid and 9 briquettes under the oven.

6. Set loaves in the pie pan, slightly separated from each other, then place pie pan in the oven on top of the trivet.

7. Replace lid and cook for about an hour, until meat loaf is brown yet moist on the inside. Refresh coals as required.

REQUIRED EQUIPMENT:
12-inch camp Dutch oven with trivet
9-inch pie pan
Large mixing bowl

Dwight Bost, Melbourne, Florida
Committee Member
Troop 285, Central Florida Council

Servings: 8–10
Preparation Time: 1½ hours
Challenge Level: Moderate

Bulgarian Black Sea Moussaka

"This is one of the various international dishes I have introduced at our Scout campouts."

PREPARATION AT CAMP:

1. Preheat Dutch oven over 25 coals.

2. Brown the ground beef and pork together in the olive oil for a few minutes, then add onion, garlic, savory, salt, black pepper, and paprika. Stir.

3. While the meat mixture continues to brown, mix eggs, yogurt or kefir, feta cheese, and flour in a medium-size mixing bowl.

4. Combine potatoes and parsley with the meat mixture in the oven.

5. Pour egg mixture over the top of the meat and potatoes then sprinkle the green onions over all.

6. Bake for about 1 hour using 17 coals on the lid and 8 briquettes under the oven, until potatoes are tender.

7. Let rest 10 minutes before serving.

REQUIRED EQUIPMENT:

12-inch camp Dutch oven
Medium-size mixing bowl

Brent Shull, Belleville, Illinois
Committee Treasurer
Troop 40, Lewis and Clark Council

¾ pound lean ground beef

½ pound ground pork

2 tablespoons olive oil

1 large red onion, finely chopped

⅓ cup crushed garlic

1 teaspoon summer savory

Salt and ground black pepper to taste

1 teaspoon paprika

4 large eggs, beaten

1½ cups plain yogurt or kefir

½ cup feta cheese

1 tablespoon all-purpose flour

4 cups potatoes, peeled and cut into ½-inch cubes

½ cup chopped fresh parsley

½ cup chopped green onion

Servings: 8–10
Preparation Time: 1¾ hours
Challenge Level: Moderate

Caribbean Spiced Ribs

3 pounds country-style pork loin ribs

½ teaspoon ground black pepper

½ teaspoon ground cayenne pepper

½ teaspoon paprika

½ teaspoon ground ginger

1 teaspoon allspice

1 teaspoon ground cinnamon

1 teaspoon garlic powder

2 teaspoons powdered mustard

2 tablespoons dry minced onion

½ cup water

1 medium onion, thinly sliced into rings

1½ cups barbecue sauce (your favorite)

"The Commissioners' staff often camps together at district and council camporees, where each of us is responsible for preparing a meal. I wanted to impress my fellow commissioners with a dish having a nice blend of spices and potent flavor. You get that in this recipe, where juice continuously bastes the ribs, producing meat that falls from the bone."

PREPARATION AT CAMP:

1. Cut each rib into pieces roughly 4 inches in length.

2. In a medium-size bowl, blend the black pepper, cayenne pepper, paprika, ginger, allspice, cinnamon, garlic powder, powdered mustard, and minced onion.

3. Thoroughly rub the spice mix onto each piece of meat.

4. Pour water into Dutch oven and layer spiced ribs and sliced onions within.

5. Cover and cook for 90 minutes using 13 coals on the lid and 12 briquettes under the oven. Refresh coals as required to maintain heat.

6. While oven remains on coals, remove lid and pour barbecue sauce over ribs.

7. Return coal-covered lid to the oven and continue cooking for an additional 15 minutes.

REQUIRED EQUIPMENT:
12-inch camp Dutch oven
Medium-size mixing bowl

C. Phillip Jones, Morrisville, North Carolina
Troop Unit Commissioner
Occoneechee Council

Servings: 8–10
Preparation Time: 2 hours
Challenge Level: Easy

Slow-Cooked Western Ribs

PREPARATION AT CAMP:

1. Preheat Dutch oven over 24 briquettes.

2. Season meat by rubbing with your choice of seasonings.

3. Brown meat in Dutch oven in the oil, 3 to 5 minutes per side. Remove meat and set aside. The ribs are only browned on the surface in this step, not cooked throughout.

4. Inside the Dutch oven, layer the remainder of the ingredients in the following order: celery, onions, ribs, tomatoes with juice, mandarin oranges with juice, barbecue sauce, and hot sauce.

5. Bake for about 4 hours using 17 coals on the lid and 7 briquettes under the oven. Refresh coals as needed.

REQUIRED EQUIPMENT:

14-inch camp Dutch oven

Cheryl Mischkulnig, Hamilton, Ohio
Public Relations Chair
Troop 923, Dan Beard Council

Cold-weather dining. SCOTT H. SIMERLY SR.

3 pounds western-style pork ribs, trimmed of fat

Meat seasoning suggestions (your choice or combination): salt, ground black pepper, onion powder, garlic powder, ancho chili powder, or New Mexico chili powder

2 tablespoons cooking oil

6–8 stalks celery, thinly sliced

3 medium-size onions, thinly sliced

1 (14½-ounce) can chopped tomatoes with green chilies (do not drain)

1 (11-ounce) can mandarin oranges (do not drain)

1 cup Sue Bee Honey Original BBQ sauce

1 cup hot sauce

Servings: 8–10
Preparation Time: 4¾ hours
Challenge Level: Moderate

Troop 31's Chicken and Dressing

1 (6-ounce) box Stove Top Cornbread Stuffing Mix

1 (14-ounce) can low-sodium chicken broth

2 stalks celery, chopped

2 teaspoons minced or pressed fresh garlic

1 (5–6 pound) whole chicken, gutted and washed

Caution: To avoid food poisoning, it is imperative when baking stuffing inside a chicken that the cooking temperature reaches a sufficiently high temperature inside the cavity. Use a food thermometer to carefully probe the cavity before taking the chicken off the coals. The temperature throughout the meat and the stuffing must be at least 165°F.

PREPARATION AT CAMP:

1. In a medium-size bowl, combine stuffing mix, chicken broth, celery, and garlic.

2. Pack stuffing inside the chicken cavity.

3. Place stuffed chicken on a trivet or rack inside Dutch oven.

4. Bake for about 1 hour and 15 minutes using 22 coals on the lid and 12 briquettes under the oven, until the chicken is cooked through.

REQUIRED EQUIPMENT:

Deep 14-inch camp Dutch oven with trivet
Medium-size mixing bowl

Delano LaGow, Oswego, Illinois
Committee Member
Troop 31, Three Fires Council

Servings: 10–12
Preparation Time: 1¾ hours
Challenge Level: Moderate

Unicoi Pizza

PREPARATION AT CAMP:

1. To prepare dough, add yeast, 2 tablespoons sugar, and warm water to a large plastic mixing bowl. Stir well then let rest for 10 minutes.

2. Gradually pour flours and ½ teaspoon salt into the bowl with the yeast water, kneading thoroughly as you go.

3. Cover bowl with plastic wrap and let dough stand about 30 minutes to rise. Bowl should be placed in a warm (not hot) location. If the day is chilly, wrap cloth towels or a sleeping bag around the bowl to retain heat.

4. In a medium-size bowl, thoroughly mix all sauce ingredients.

5. Line the Dutch oven with heavy-duty aluminum foil and grease the foil.

6. Flatten the risen dough across the bottom of oven and slightly up the wall.

7. Spread sauce evenly over dough.

8. Add your favorite toppings and cover all with cheese.

9. Bake using 26 coals on the lid and 13 briquettes under the bottom. After 20 minutes, begin checking every 5 minutes for cheese to melt. Once cheese is thoroughly melted, remove the oven from heat.

10. Remove lid from oven and allow pizza to rest until cheese begins to re-solidify.

11. Pizza can now be sliced and served.

REQUIRED EQUIPMENT:

16-inch camp Dutch oven
Large plastic mixing bowl
Medium-size mixing bowl
Plastic wrap
Heavy-duty aluminum foil

Tim Conners, Statesboro, Georgia
Assistant Scoutmaster
Troop 340, Coastal Empire Council

Christine Conners, Statesboro, Georgia
Committee Member and Merit Badge Counselor
Troop 340, Coastal Empire Council

DOUGH INGREDIENTS:

1 (1¼-ounce) envelope rapid-rise yeast

2 tablespoons sugar

2 cups warm (120–130°F) water

2 cups all-purpose flour

2 cups whole wheat flour

½ teaspoon salt

SAUCE INGREDIENTS:

1 (15-ounce) can tomato sauce

1 (12-ounce) can tomato paste

½ teaspoon powdered garlic

1½ teaspoons Italian seasoning blend

¼ teaspoon salt

2 teaspoons sugar

2 tablespoons olive oil

1 cup water

Favorite toppings, such as bell pepper, onions, tomatoes, pineapple, black or green olives, mushrooms, pepperoni, salami, ham, cooked sausage, or cooked chicken

8 ounces (2 cups) shredded cheese (your favorite)

Servings: 10–12
Preparation Time: 1¾ hours
Challenge Level: Difficult

Camp Gorman Beef Stroganoff

2 pounds flank steak or roast, sliced and cut into bite-size pieces

4 tablespoons vegetable oil

1 small onion, chopped

8 ounces sliced fresh mushrooms

2 (0.87-ounce) packages McCormick Brown Gravy mix

2 cups water

Celery salt and ground black pepper to taste

1 (16-ounce) bag egg noodles

1 (16-ounce) container sour cream

Options: Cooking time can be extended to up to 3 hours total. The longer the cooking time, the more tender the meat will become.

Goes great with broccoli.

PREPARATION AT CAMP:

1. Preheat Dutch oven over 25 coals.

2. Brown the meat in 3 tablespoons oil for about 5 minutes.

3. Add onions and mushrooms. Sauté until onions become translucent.

4. Pour brown gravy mix and water into the oven. Stir to blend.

5. Add celery salt and black pepper to taste.

6. Place lid on oven, then remove about 10 of the coals from under the oven. No coals should be on lid.

7. Continue to cook on low heat for a minimum of 1½ hours, refreshing briquettes as required.

8. About an hour after placing the lid on the oven, prepare the egg noodles in a medium-size cook pot per package directions, adding a tablespoon of oil to the boiling water to prevent noodles from sticking.

9. Drain noodles then remove stroganoff from heat.

10. Blend sour cream into stroganoff and serve over noodles.

REQUIRED EQUIPMENT:

12-inch camp Dutch oven
Medium-size cook pot

Carl Wust Jr., Conyers, Georgia
Scoutmaster
Troop 410, Atlanta Area Council

Servings: 10–12
Preparation Time: 2¼ hours
Challenge Level: Moderate

Camp Coppersnake Beef Stew

"I began making this stew about 35 years ago, in Dutch ovens and roasters. My troop held its own summer camp for a few years at a place in West Virginia called Camp Coppersnake, where I occasionally prepared this dish."

PREPARATION AT CAMP:

1. Preheat Dutch oven over 23 coals and warm the oil.

2. In a large bowl, mix together bread crumbs, garlic powder, black pepper, and salt.

3. Add cubed meat to the bowl and toss to coat.

4. Brown the coated meat on all sides in the now-hot Dutch oven.

5. Add about half of the can of beef broth to the oven along with the bay leaf and carrots.

6. Layer sliced onions in the oven and add potatoes. Pour tomato sauce over everything then add the remaining beef broth. Place cover on oven.

7. Using 16 coals on the lid and 7 briquettes under the oven, cook for 1½ hours. Refresh coals as required and stir occasionally.

8. Add green beans and continue cooking for an additional 20 minutes.

REQUIRED EQUIPMENT:

12-inch camp Dutch oven
Large mixing bowl

George Svec, Dravosburg, Pennsylvania
Assistant Scoutmaster
Troop 54, Greater Pittsburgh Council

2 tablespoons vegetable oil

½ cup Progresso Italian Style bread crumbs

2 tablespoons garlic powder

1 teaspoon ground black pepper

1 teaspoon salt

2 pounds stewing beef or chuck roast, cut into 1-inch cubes

1 (14½-ounce) can beef broth

1 bay leaf

6 large carrots, peeled and cut into 1-inch pieces

1 medium onion, sliced

6 medium potatoes, peeled and quartered

1 (8-ounce) can tomato sauce

8 ounces frozen green beans, thawed

Option: Goes great with biscuits.

Servings: 10–12
Preparation Time: 2½ hours
Challenge Level: Moderate

2 pounds lean ground beef

2 (8.8-ounce) packages Uncle Ben's Spanish Style Ready Rice

2 (10-ounce) cans green enchilada sauce

1 cup milk

1 (4-ounce) container Egg Beaters

1 cup Bisquick baking mix

8 ounces (2 cups) shredded cheese, divided

1 (16-ounce) jar salsa (your favorite)

1 (8-ounce) container sour cream

Option: Serve with slaw, peach cobbler, and lemonade.

Meramec River Chili Pie

"This recipe is very popular with the adult Scouters. It's one of my oldest recipes. I first served it to my troop on a chilly, damp evening after a day of canoeing on the Meramec River in Missouri. Some warm food with a little spicy kick was the perfect way to end the day."

PREPARATION AT CAMP:

1. Preheat Dutch oven over 25 coals.

2. Brown the ground beef.

3. Add rice and enchilada sauce to the warm ground beef. Stir.

4. Mix milk, Egg Beaters, Bisquick, and ½ cup cheese in a medium-size bowl.

5. Place remaining cheese over meat and rice mixture in the oven.

6. Slowly pour or spoon out the Bisquick mixture evenly on top of the cheese. Do not pour too fast nor mix the ingredients once they are in the oven. The goal here is to make a cheese biscuit topping.

7. Using 15 coals on the lid and 10 briquettes under the oven, bake for about 30 minutes, until the top is golden. Refresh coals if required.

8. Serve with salsa and sour cream.

REQUIRED EQUIPMENT:
12-inch camp Dutch oven
Medium-size mixing bowl

Emery Corley, St. Louis, Missouri
Assistant Scoutmaster
Troop 809, Greater Saint Louis Area Council

Servings: 12–14
Preparation Time: 1¼ hours
Challenge Level: Easy

The Life Scout's Lazy Lasagna

"The boys, including my son Luke, a Life Scout, love to have lasagna on our campouts. But they don't like all the preparation that can be required. So I came up with this easy and quick substitute for traditional lasagna, and it has been a hit and a regular ever since. For an even easier cleanup, we use the Dutch oven foil liner pans that can be found online and at local sporting good stores, making this a truly 'Lazy' Lasagna."

PREPARATION AT CAMP:

1. Preheat Dutch oven over 27 coals.

2. Cook sausage in oven until it is no longer pink. Set aside.

3. Coat bottom of oven with about 1 cup of pasta sauce.

4. Distribute 1 bag of cheese ravioli over the sauce then add a layer of about half of the cooked Italian Sausage.

5. Pour can of Italian diced tomatoes over the sausage then distribute the second bag of cheese ravioli over the tomatoes.

6. Spread the remainder of the sausage over the ravioli followed by the rest of the pasta sauce.

7. Bake for about 45 minutes using 18 coals on the lid and 9 briquettes under the oven. Refresh coals as required.

8. Remove lid, add shredded cheese, replace lid, and cook for an additional 15 minutes.

REQUIRED EQUIPMENT:

12-inch camp Dutch oven

Tracy Tuttle, Boise, Idaho
Den Leader
Pack 97, Ore-Ida Council

1 pound ground Italian sausage (sweet or spicy)

1 (26-ounce) jar pasta sauce (your favorite)

2 (24-ounce) bags frozen cheese ravioli, thawed

1 (14½-ounce) can Italian diced tomatoes (with basil, garlic, and oregano)

1 pound (4 cups) shredded mozzarella or Italian blend cheese

Servings: 12–14
Preparation Time: 1¾ hours
Challenge Level: Easy

Mixed-Bag Baked Beans

2 pounds bacon

1 large onion, chopped

1 cup brown sugar

1 cup white vinegar

2 teaspoons garlic salt

2 teaspoons
ground mustard

1 (28-ounce) can
pork and beans

1 (16-ounce) can
kidney beans, drained

1 (16-ounce) can
garbanzo beans, drained

1 (16-ounce) can
lima beans, drained

1 (16-ounce) can
butter beans, drained

"When a bean recipe starts with bacon, it has to be good. There is no exception to that rule here. And everyone who likes beans knows they come out even better when cooked in cast iron. This recipe is adapted from a family favorite that my mother made when I was of Cub Scout age. Stick-to-the-ribs filling!"

PREPARATION AT CAMP:

1. Preheat Dutch oven over 25 coals.

2. Fry bacon in preheated Dutch oven. Remove bacon before it becomes crispy. Chop and set aside in medium-size bowl.

3. Carefully drain all but about 1 tablespoon of grease from the oven. Brown onions in the hot oven then add to the bacon in the bowl.

4. Pour brown sugar, vinegar, garlic salt, and ground mustard into the oven. Stir well, then let simmer for 10 minutes.

5. Add all the beans to the Dutch oven along with the bacon and onions, previously set aside. Stir.

6. Bake for 1 hour using 17 coals on the lid and 8 briquettes under the oven. Refresh coals as required.

REQUIRED EQUIPMENT:

12-inch camp Dutch oven
Medium-size mixing bowl

Brett Morehead, Ardmore, Oklahoma
Scoutmaster
Troop 5, Arbuckle Area Council

Servings: 12–14
Preparation Time: 2 hours
Challenge Level: Moderate

Mexican Lasagna

PREPARATION AT CAMP:

1. Preheat Dutch oven over 25 coals.

2. Brown ground beef in the oven, then transfer meat to a large mixing bowl. Remove oven from heat.

3. To the beef, add the taco seasoning mix, beans, and spaghetti sauce. Mix.

4. Spread about a third of the beef-sauce mixture on the bottom of the oven.

5. Top mixture with 4 tortillas, covering as much of the surface of the beef-sauce as possible.

6. Spread another third of the beef-sauce on the tortillas then distribute about a third of the shredded cheese across the top.

7. Continue layering with another 4 tortillas, the remainder of the beef-sauce mix, and another third of the cheese.

8. Finish with a final layer of 4 tortillas covered with the remainder of the cheese.

9. Bake for about 30 minutes, using 17 coals on the lid and 8 briquettes under the oven, until heated through. Refresh coals if required.

REQUIRED EQUIPMENT:

12-inch camp Dutch oven
Large mixing bowl

William Younts, Mooresville, North Carolina
Assistant Scoutmaster
Troop 377, Piedmont Council

1½ pounds lean ground beef

2 (1-ounce) packages taco seasoning mix

2 (15-ounce) cans pinto, kidney, or black beans, drained

2 (26-ounce) cans spaghetti sauce

1 dozen corn tortillas

1½ pounds shredded cheese

Servings: 14–16
Preparation Time: 1¼ hours
Challenge Level: Easy

8 skinless boneless chicken breasts

1 red bell pepper, seeded and halved

1 green bell pepper, seeded and halved

2 (15-ounce) cans whole tomatoes, drained and chopped

2 medium onions, finely chopped

3 cloves garlic, minced

3 (10-ounce) cans enchilada sauce

2 (4-ounce) cans chopped mild green chilies, drained

2 cups water

1 (15-ounce) can chicken broth

1 (15-ounce) can beef broth

2 teaspoons ground cumin

1 tablespoon chili powder

2 teaspoons ground black pepper

1 teaspoon ground cayenne pepper

1 teaspoon salt

1 bay leaf

2 cups shredded Colby-Monterey Jack cheese blend

1 bag (about 14 ounces) tortilla chips

¼ cup grated Parmesan cheese

1 medium avocado, peeled and diced (optional)

1 (16-ounce) container sour cream (optional)

Servings: 14–16
Preparation Time: 2½ hours
Challenge Level: Difficult

Spicy Tortilla Soup

"This hearty dish packs a kick, developing a deep, thick richness while simmering for hours. The recipe requires little in the way of equipment, but allow for a lot of time from meat-on-grill to serving time, as this is slow camp cooking at its finest. Spicy Tortilla Soup was awarded first place in the entree category in *Scouting* magazine's 2009 Great Tastes in Camp Cooking contest."

PREPARATION AT CAMP:

1. Grill chicken, preferably over an open fire, browning each piece on both sides. The meat does not require thorough heating during this step because it will finish cooking once in the Dutch oven.

2. Roast red and green bell pepper halves on the grill until lightly charred.

3. Cube the grilled chicken breasts into bite-size pieces and chop the grilled peppers.

4. Place chicken and peppers, along with the tomatoes, onions, and garlic, in Dutch oven. Add enchilada sauce and green chilies.

5. Pour water, chicken broth, and beef broth into Dutch oven. Stir, then add cumin, chili powder, black pepper, cayenne pepper, salt, and bay leaf. Stir thoroughly.

6. Cover and cook for 2 hours using 10 coals on the lid and 20 briquettes under the oven. Refresh the coals as they expire.

7. Remove from heat and stir the shredded cheese into the soup.

8. Serve in bowls, topping with a handful of crushed tortilla chips and a sprinkling of Parmesan cheese.

9. Garnish with optional diced avocado and a dollop of sour cream.

REQUIRED EQUIPMENT:
12-inch camp Dutch oven

Mac McCoy, Hanford, California
Assistant District Commissioner
Sequoia Council

Camp Mack
Ham Loaf and Cheese

"This recipe is named in honor of the J. E. Mack Scout Reservation."

PREPARATION AT CAMP:

1. Fill a medium-size pot about half-full with water and boil the macaroni to al dente (slightly firm) over high heat.

2. While the macaroni is cooking, layer about two-thirds of the ham loaf slices in the bottom of the Dutch oven.

3. Mold the loaf slices to an even depth across the entire bottom of oven. Loaf layer should be about ¾ inch thick.

4. Add a layer of cooked macaroni about 1 inch thick over the loaf followed by a layer of grated cheese.

5. Add another layer of macaroni, then cheese, and keep layering until no macaroni remains. Reserve enough cheese to cover the final layer of macaroni.

6. Add remaining ham loaf slices to the top of the macaroni.

7. Bake for about 1 hour using 18 coals on the lid and 9 briquettes under the oven, until ham loaf is fully cooked and the cheese is melted. Refresh coals as required.

REQUIRED EQUIPMENT:

12-inch camp Dutch oven
Medium-size cook pot

Derrick Tryon, Ephrata, Pennsylvania
Eagle Scout and Scoutmaster
Troop 70, Pennsylvania Dutch Council

1 (1-pound) box macaroni pasta

4 pounds ham loaf, sliced about ¾-inch thick

2 (10-ounce) blocks Kraft Cracker Barrel Extra Sharp White cheddar cheese, grated

TIP:
Ham loaf is similar to meat loaf except that it is made with pork. This specialty item can be found in most meat markets.

Servings: 18–20
Preparation Time: 1½ hours
Challenge Level: Easy

8 cloves garlic, chopped fine

1 Vidalia or sweet onion, chopped fine

2 tablespoons olive oil

3 pounds frozen precooked un-breaded chicken, cut up into ½-inch pieces

3 (14½-ounce) cans cannellini beans, drained and rinsed

1 (14½-ounce) can white corn, drained

2 (15-ounce) jars Alfredo sauce

1 (14½-ounce) can low-sodium chicken broth

2 teaspoons ground coriander seed

1 tablespoon ground cilantro leaves

½ teaspoon garlic powder

½ teaspoon ground black pepper

1 tablespoon chili powder

½ tablespoon Texas Pete hot sauce

½ teaspoon Tabasco sauce

½ teaspoon crushed red pepper

1 tablespoon cumin

2–3 Anaheim chili peppers, chopped fine

1 pound finely shredded sharp cheddar cheese

Servings: 18–20
Preparation Time: 1½ hours
Challenge Level: Moderate

Occoneechee Spicy White Chili

PREPARATION AT CAMP:

1. Preheat Dutch oven over 32 coals.

2. Sauté garlic and onion in oil.

3. Add chicken, beans, corn, Alfredo sauce, chicken broth, coriander, cilantro, garlic powder, black pepper, chili powder, hot sauces, crushed red pepper, cumin, and Anaheim peppers. Stir well.

4. Cook for about 30 minutes using 21 coals on the lid and 11 briquettes under the oven. Refresh coals as required.

5. Stir the chili, replace the lid, and continue to cook for 15 more minutes.

6. Serve in bowls and top with cheese.

REQUIRED EQUIPMENT:

14-inch camp Dutch oven

Andrew Gilbert, Raleigh, North Carolina
District Commissioner
Falls District, Occoneechee Council

Option: Goes great with buttered Italian bread. Wrap the bread in heavy-duty foil and place on coals on top of the Dutch oven to warm.

Scoutmaster's Lasagna

PREPARATION AT CAMP:

1. Preheat Dutch oven over 32 coals.

2. Brown beef, garlic, and onion in oven then transfer to a large bowl. Remove oven from heat.

3. Add spaghetti sauce, salt, black pepper, and Italian seasoning blend to the beef-onion mix and stir well.

4. Mix ricotta cheese and eggs in a medium-size bowl and set aside.

5. Carefully line hot oven with aluminum foil.

6. Spread about a third of the beef mixture on the bottom of the oven. Next add a layer of about a third of the noodles followed by about a third of the ricotta-egg mixture and a third of the mozzarella cheese.

7. Repeat this order 2 more times until all ingredients are layered, ending with a layer of mozzarella cheese.

8. Cook for about 45 minutes using 21 coals on the lid and 11 briquettes under the oven, until noodles are thoroughly cooked. Refresh coals as required.

REQUIRED EQUIPMENT:

14-inch camp Dutch oven
Large mixing bowl
Medium-size mixing bowl
Heavy-duty aluminum foil

Dwayne Fair, Newbern, Tennessee
Scoutmaster
Troop 386, West Tennessee Area Council

2 pounds lean ground beef

2 teaspoons minced garlic

1 large onion, chopped

2 (26-ounce) jars spaghetti sauce

½ teaspoon salt

½ teaspoon ground black pepper

2 teaspoons Italian seasoning blend

2 (15-ounce) tubs ricotta cheese

2 eggs

1 (16-ounce) box lasagna noodles, uncooked

1½ pounds (6 cups) mozzarella cheese

TIPS:
- Some of the noodles will need to be broken to all fit in the oven and fully cover the layer of beef.
- The noodles soften during the baking process by absorbing moisture from the wet ingredients.
- Be sure the noodles are adequately covered by moist ingredients on all sides and not exposed directly to the air; otherwise, they may not soften completely.

Servings: 18–20
Preparation Time: 1¾ hours
Challenge Level: Moderate

1½ pounds fresh green beans, stems removed and rinsed

1 fresh garlic clove, minced

½ cup water

2 tablespoons butter

Option: This dish goes great with pork roast and dumplings.

Green Beans and Garlic

PREPARATION AT CAMP:

1. Place beans in Dutch oven and add garlic and water.

2. Cover and cook over 25 coals for about 15 minutes, until green beans are warm and tender. No coals are used on the lid.

3. Carefully drain water.

4. Add butter to top of warm beans and let melt before serving.

REQUIRED EQUIPMENT:

12-inch camp Dutch oven

Bob Slowikowski, Plainfield, Illinois
Webelos Den Leader
Pack 85, Rainbow Council

Servings: 4–6
Preparation Time: ¾ hour
Challenge Level: Easy

Poppa's Jalapeño Poppers

"Removing the seeds and veins usually reduces the heat from jalapeños, leaving just the flavor behind. But it's like Russian roulette, because you still occasionally get a hot one. First time I made these, I had my daughter bring some over to my neighbor, Brian, for his approval. Must've left a seed in because he got the atomic one. My daughter said he blew fire from his mouth and smoke from his ears."

PREPARATION AT CAMP:

1. Spread cream cheese into each of the pepper halves.

2. Wrap each pepper half with a half-strip of bacon and secure with a toothpick.

3. Fashion a plate from the heavy-duty foil and set over the trivet in the Dutch oven.

4. Cook for 45 minutes using 15 coals on the lid and 10 briquettes under the oven.

REQUIRED EQUIPMENT:

12-inch camp Dutch oven with trivet
Heavy-duty aluminum foil
Toothpicks

John Foster, Duchesne, Utah
District Commissioner
Kings Peak District, Utah National Parks Council

1 (8-ounce) package cream cheese

12 jalapeño peppers, sliced in half lengthwise and seeded

1 pound bacon, each strip sliced in half

TIPS:
• Wear food service-type gloves when handling hot peppers like jalapeños to avoid irritating your skin or, later, accidentally carrying the hot pepper oil to your eyes.
• A small wire rack can be used in place of the foil plate and trivet.

Servings: 6 (4 poppers each)
Preparation Time: 1 hour
Challenge Level: Easy

Den Leader's German Potato Salad

"Best side dish ever!"

4–6 strips precooked bacon, chopped

1 onion, diced

1 (10¾-ounce) can condensed cream of celery soup

¾ cup water (or a soup can about half-full)

3 tablespoons white vinegar

1 teaspoon sugar

¼ teaspoon salt

⅛ teaspoon ground black pepper

1 (30-ounce) bag frozen shredded hash browns, thawed

PREPARATION AT CAMP:

1. In a small bowl, combine bacon, onion, soup, water, vinegar, sugar, salt, and black pepper.

2. Distribute hash browns in the bottom of Dutch oven.

3. Pour soup mixture over potatoes.

4. Bake for about 1 hour using 18 coals on the lid and 9 briquettes under the oven. Refresh coals as required.

REQUIRED EQUIPMENT:
12-inch camp Dutch oven
Small mixing bowl

Tracy Tuttle, Boise, Idaho
Den Leader
Pack 97, Ore-Ida Council

Making the side dishes... *SCOTT H. SIMERLY SR.*

Servings: 6–8
Preparation Time: 1¼ hours
Challenge Level: Easy

Twice-Baked Potatoes

PREPARATION AT CAMP:

1. Coat the potatoes in vegetable oil and carefully poke holes throughout each with a knife or fork.

2. Bake potatoes in Dutch oven for an hour using 17 coals on the lid and 8 briquettes under the oven. Refresh coals as required.

3. In a large mixing bowl, blend together sour cream, butter, black pepper, salt, milk, half of the diced green onions, and half of the shredded cheese.

4. Once the potatoes have finished baking, remove from oven and allow them to cool for about 15 minutes. Keep oven over coals.

5. Cut each potato in half lengthwise. Scoop the insides of each into the bowl containing the sour cream mix, being careful not to break the skins. Blend the potato mixture well.

6. Spoon mixture back into the potato skins, return the potatoes to the oven, replace the lid, and bake for about 15 more minutes. Refresh coals if necessary.

7. Once finished, sprinkle each potato with bacon bits and remaining cheese and diced green onions.

REQUIRED EQUIPMENT:
12-inch camp Dutch oven
Large mixing bowl

David and Janet Stanger, Boise, Idaho
Committee Members
Crew 60, Ore-Ida Council

4 russet potatoes, cleaned and scrubbed

Vegetable oil to rub on outside of potatoes

1 cup sour cream

¼ cup (½ standard stick) butter

½ teaspoon ground black pepper

½ teaspoon salt

½ cup milk

8 green onions, trimmed and diced

4 ounces (1 cup) shredded cheese

¼ cup bacon bits

Servings: 8
Preparation Time: 2¼ hours
Challenge Level: Moderate

2 tablespoons olive oil

2 tablespoons butter

¼ cup finely chopped onion

¼ cup chopped fresh garlic

2 cups uncooked Arborio rice (or regular long grain rice)

1 (48-ounce) container chicken broth

Salt and ground black pepper to taste

½ cup grated Parmesan cheese

TIP:
Half of a 4½-ounce jar of minced garlic is equivalent to ¼ cup of fresh chopped garlic.

Servings: 8–10
Preparation Time: 1 hour
Challenge Level: Easy

Tony's Risotto

"This is a favorite Italian dish that I prepare at home at least once each week. So, naturally, I started fixing it at camp for the troop as well. I named it for my son Tony who is the reason I became involved with Boy Scouts nearly 20 years ago."

PREPARATION AT CAMP:

1. Combine olive oil, butter, onion, garlic, rice, and broth in Dutch oven. Stir.

2. Bake for 30 to 40 minutes using 17 coals on the lid and 8 briquettes under the oven, until water is absorbed.

3. Once off the coals, add salt and black pepper to taste and sprinkle with cheese. Allow cheese to melt before serving.

REQUIRED EQUIPMENT:

12-inch camp Dutch oven

Beverly Jo Antonini, Morgantown, West Virginia
Assistant Scoutmaster
Troop 49, Mountaineer Area Council

Campout Fried Rice

"As avid campers and lovers of good Chinese takeout, my troop brought fried rice to the woods. Use it as a side dish with other take-out favorites . . . Egg rolls, anyone?"

PREPARATION AT HOME:

1. Cook rice in medium-size pot according to package directions to produce 5 cups.

2. Allow rice to cool, then package in a heavy-duty ziplock bag for camp. Keep refrigerated until needed.

PREPARATION AT CAMP:

1. Preheat Dutch oven over 25 coals.

2. Carefully add oil, garlic, and pepper flakes to the hot oven and stir, sautéing the garlic.

3. When the garlic begins to turn a light brown, add the veggies. Quickly stir-fry using a wooden spoon or spatula. Crunchy veggies are better than mushy.

4. Remove vegetables and set aside in a medium-size bowl, leaving any oil in the oven.

5. Remove about a third of the coals from under the oven to reduce heat.

6. Add the previously cooked rice to the oven and any remaining unheated oil as needed, stirring gently.

7. Once the rice is hot throughout, crack the eggs into the rice, quickly scrambling the eggs and rice together.

8. Once eggs are cooked, blend in the soy sauce then return the cooked vegetables to the oven.

9. Toss the mixture together and serve hot.

REQUIRED EQUIPMENT:

12-inch camp Dutch oven
Medium-size bowl

Andy Mills, Bridgewater, Massachusetts
Eagle Scout and Assistant Scoutmaster
Troop 4480, Old Colony Council

5 cups cooked white rice

½ cup sesame oil

4 garlic cloves, minced

Dash of red pepper flakes (more, if additional heat is desired)

4 cups chopped (½ to 1½ inches in length) fresh veggies, using what's in season: spring onions, bell peppers, pea pods, bok choy, cabbage, green peas, regular onions, carrots, bean sprouts, mushrooms, broccoli, or zucchini

2 eggs

⅔ cup low-salt or regular soy sauce

Option: Add cooked chicken, shrimp, beef, or pork in Step 9 for a full meal.

TIP:
The rice can also be cooked in camp using a medium-size pot. Regardless of how it's prepared, be sure the rice is only damp and not wet before using in Step 7. Otherwise, it could turn mushy during final cooking. Pat the rice dry using paper towels if need be, and make sure the oil is hot.

Servings: 8–10
Preparation Time: 1 hour
Challenge Level: Moderate

Ken's Scalloped Corn

1 (14½-ounce) can creamed corn

½ cup (1 standard stick) butter, softened

1 (15-ounce) can whole kernel corn (do not drain)

1 (8-ounce) container sour cream

2 eggs, lightly beaten

½ teaspoon chili powder (optional)

1 (4-ounce) can diced green chilies (optional)

1 (8½-ounce) box Jiffy corn muffin mix

PREPARATION AT CAMP:

1. Combine all ingredients except corn muffin mix in a large mixing bowl. For a little heat, optional chili powder and green chilies can also be added at this time.

2. Gradually add corn muffin mix to bowl and stir thoroughly to combine.

3. Pour mixture into greased Dutch oven.

4. Using 16 coals on the lid and 7 briquettes under the oven, bake 50 minutes, until the top is firm and golden. Refresh coals as needed.

REQUIRED EQUIPMENT:

12-inch camp Dutch oven
Large mixing bowl

Ken Vetrovec, Racine, Wisconsin
Eagle Scout and Woodbadge Coordinator
Troop 634, Southeast Wisconsin Council

He's either saving the best for last or someone doesn't like his vegetables. *SCOTT H. SIMERLY SR.*

Servings: 8–10
Preparation Time: 1¼ hours
Challenge Level: Easy

Rip-Roaring Onions au Gratin

"Just like Momma never made. Yes, even kids who turn their noses up at onions will like this . . . once they taste it. The onions really mellow during cooking, especially if Vidalias are used. It makes for a side that most have never had before. But a word of caution: Eating this many onions in a single setting can make for a rip-roaring time."

2 tablespoons butter

8–10 medium white sweet or Vidalia onions, sliced thin and separated into rings

⅔ cup Bisquick baking mix

¼ teaspoon cayenne pepper

12 ounces (3 cups) shredded cheddar cheese

PREPARATION AT CAMP:

1. Melt butter in Dutch oven over 25 coals.

2. Add onions to the oven and sauté until tender.

3. In a medium-size mixing bowl, combine Bisquick, cayenne pepper, and 2 cups shredded cheese. Add this to the onions in the oven and stir well to coat.

4. Bake for 20 minutes, using 17 coals on the lid and 8 briquettes under the oven.

5. Remove lid and add the remaining 1 cup of shredded cheese to the top of the onions.

6. Replace lid and allow to cook for about 10 more minutes, until cheese is fully melted.

7. Serve immediately.

REQUIRED EQUIPMENT:

12-inch camp Dutch oven
Medium-size mixing bowl

Tom Cartwright, Euclid, Ohio
Cubmaster
Pack 143, Greater Cleveland Council

Servings: 12–14
Preparation Time: 1¼ hours
Challenge Level: Easy

2 pounds elbow macaroni pasta

⅛ cup (¼ standard stick) butter

1 (16-ounce) package Velveeta cheese, cubed

1 pound white American cheese, cubed

½ cup milk

2 tablespoons spicy brown mustard

Crew 2's Mac and Cheese

"Don't rush this recipe, because once it's finished cooking, it is the best mac 'n' cheese ever. Our Crew licks the foil clean, it's that awesome. Crew 2 promises that no hungry Scout will pass this up."

PREPARATION AT CAMP:

1. In a large cook pot, boil pasta in 6 to 8 quarts of water until tender then drain and rinse.

2. Line the Dutch oven with foil then liberally grease the lining with butter.

3. Dump about half of the pasta in the oven.

4. Distribute half of the Velveeta and American cheese cubes over the pasta.

5. Top the cheese with the remainder of the pasta then cover the pasta with the remainder of the cheese.

6. Combine milk with mustard in a cup then pour over cheese in the oven.

7. Bake for about 1½ hours using 21 coals on the lid and 11 briquettes under the oven. Refresh coals as required.

REQUIRED EQUIPMENT:

14-inch camp Dutch oven
Large cook pot
Heavy-duty aluminum foil

Ariane Racow, Cheshire, Connecticut
Assistant Adviser
Crew 2, Connecticut Rivers Council

TIPS:
To save time at camp, the pasta can be prepared and packaged at home. White American cheese can often be found in the deli, if not on the grocery shelves.

Servings: 12–14
Preparation Time: 2 hours
Challenge Level: Easy

Texas Beans

PREPARATION AT CAMP:

1. Preheat Dutch oven over 25 coals.

2. Fry bacon in oven.

3. Add onion rings and cook until onions are translucent.

4. Add garlic powder, powdered mustard, vinegar, and brown sugar. Stir.

5. Cook for 20 minutes then stir in the beans.

6. Cover and bake for about 30 minutes, using 17 coals on the lid and 8 briquettes under the oven. Refresh coals as required.

REQUIRED EQUIPMENT:

12-inch camp Dutch oven

Dwayne Fair, Newbern, Tennessee
Scoutmaster
Troop 386, West Tennessee Area Council

1 pound bacon, diced

6–8 large onions, cut into rings

½ teaspoon garlic powder

½ teaspoon powdered mustard

1 cup white vinegar

1½ cups brown sugar

1 (15¼-ounce) can lima beans, drained

2 (16-ounce) cans kidney beans, drained

2 (28-ounce) cans pork and beans

Servings: 14–16
Preparation Time: 1½ hours
Challenge Level: Easy

¼ cup (½ standard stick) butter, softened

1 egg

½ cup granulated sugar

1 cup milk

1½ cups all-purpose flour

½ teaspoon salt

2 teaspoons baking powder

1 cup cornmeal

Camp Tahosa Corn Bread

"This is my Mom's scratch corn bread recipe that I adapted for the Dutch oven. It makes for a great accompaniment to chilis, stews, and soups. This recipe won third place in *Scouting* magazine's 2009 Great Tastes in Camp Cooking contest."

PREPARATION AT CAMP:

1. In a medium-size bowl, blend butter, egg, and sugar.

2. Add milk, flour, salt, baking powder, and cornmeal. Mix thoroughly.

3. Pour batter into greased Dutch oven.

4. Bake using 19 coals on the lid and 10 briquettes under the oven for 10 minutes.

5. Reduce heat by removing 2 coals from the lid, then continue baking for about 20 additional minutes, until an inserted toothpick comes out clean.

REQUIRED EQUIPMENT:

12-inch camp Dutch oven
Medium-size mixing bowl

Mike Gill, Brighton, Colorado
Eagle Scout, Cubmaster, and Assistant Scoutmaster
Pack 564 / Troop 564, Denver Area Council

Servings: 6–8
Preparation Time: 1 hour
Challenge Level: Easy

Nutty Bread Gone Bananas

PREPARATION AT CAMP:

1. Preheat Dutch oven using 21 coals on the lid and 11 briquettes under the oven.

2. Mix oil, nutmeg, vanilla extract, and sugar together in a large bowl.

3. Blend in eggs, milk, and bananas.

4. Add baking soda, baking powder, and salt, then stir well.

5. Gradually add flour to bowl, mix thoroughly, then fold in chopped nuts.

6. Pour flour mixture into loaf pan, and place on a trivet in the Dutch oven.

7. Bake for about 1 hour, refreshing coals as needed, until toothpick or fork comes out clean.

REQUIRED EQUIPMENT:

14-inch camp Dutch oven with trivet
Large mixing bowl
9 x 5 x 3-inch loaf pan

Jason Cagle, Jacksonville, Florida
Assistant Scoutmaster
Troop 169, North Florida Council

½ cup vegetable oil

1 teaspoon ground nutmeg

½ teaspoon vanilla extract

1 cup granulated sugar

2 large eggs, lightly beaten

3 tablespoons milk

3 overripe bananas, mashed

1 teaspoon baking soda

½ teaspoon baking powder

½ teaspoon salt

2 cups all-purpose flour

½ cup chopped pecans or walnuts

Option: For an even healthier option, replace vegetable oil with applesauce.

Servings: 6–8
Preparation Time: 1¼ hours
Challenge Level: Easy

Breckenridge Broccoli Corn Bread

"This recipe is a sneaky and delicious way to slip the Scouts some vegetables."

1 (15-ounce) box Krusteaz corn bread mix

1 (14-ounce) bag frozen broccoli, thawed and finely chopped

⅔ cup milk

1 small onion, chopped

4 ounces (1 cup) shredded sharp cheddar cheese

2 eggs

½ cup (1 standard stick) butter, softened

PREPARATION AT CAMP:

1. Line Dutch oven with heavy-duty aluminum foil. Grease foil.

2. Mix all ingredients together in a large bowl. Pour batter into oven.

3. Bake for 35 to 45 minutes, using 19 coals on the lid and 10 briquettes under the oven, until the top of the bread becomes a golden brown.

REQUIRED EQUIPMENT:

12-inch camp Dutch oven
Large mixing bowl
Heavy-duty aluminum foil

Tim Conners, Statesboro, Georgia
Assistant Scoutmaster
Troop 340, Coastal Empire Council

Christine Conners, Statesboro, Georgia
Committee Member and Merit Badge Counselor
Troop 340, Coastal Empire Council

Servings: 8–10
Preparation Time: 1 hour
Challenge Level: Easy

Broccoli in the cornbread? You bet! *CHRISTINE CONNERS*

Dutch Oven Cheesy Potato Bread

PREPARATION AT CAMP:

1. Six to 8 hours before bread is to be baked, combine potato flakes, sugar, yeast, milk, butter, cheese, and onion salt in a large mixing bowl.

2. Gradually blend in the flour. The dough should be slightly sticky. If it is too sticky, add flour in very small amounts to reduce the tackiness.

3. Knead dough for about 10 minutes.

4. Wipe mixing bowl clean and place dough ball in the bowl, cover with plastic wrap, and set in a warm location.

5. Allow dough to rest until it doubles in bulk. Punch down the dough ball in the middle and then re-smooth it into a rounded disc shape.

6. Place shaped dough into greased Dutch oven. Allow dough to further rest until it doubles in bulk once more. Patience is needed here because steps 5 and 6 will take many hours.

7. Bake for about 30 minutes using 14 coals placed in a ring around the rim of the lid and 7 briquettes placed under the oven in a circle around the outer edge of the bottom.

8. After 30 minutes, remove charcoal briquettes from under the oven and continue cooking with top-heat only for about 15 minutes more.

9. Remove loaf from Dutch oven and slice to serve.

REQUIRED EQUIPMENT:
10-inch camp Dutch oven
Large plastic mixing bowl
Plastic wrap

John Malachowski, Stewartstown, Pennsylvania
Scoutmaster
Troop 27, New Birth of Freedom Council

1 cup dried potato flakes

2 tablespoons granulated sugar

1 teaspoon active dry yeast

2¼ cups lukewarm milk

1 tablespoon butter, softened

4 ounces (1 cup) shredded cheddar cheese

1 teaspoon onion salt

3 cups all-purpose flour

TIPS:
• It takes the dough a total of 6 to 8 hours to properly rise for this recipe. One approach is to prepare it the night before and let it rise overnight. Then in the morning, punch it down, and let it rise again for a couple more hours. It will be ready to bake by lunch.
• For yeast to work properly, the temperature is crucial. Temperatures above 110°F will begin to kill active dry yeast. Too cool, and the yeast won't activate, and the bread will be dense.

Servings: 8–10
Preparation Time: 1¼ hours (plus 6–8 hours of rising time)
Challenge Level: Moderate

Capirotada
(aka Spotted Dog)

6 slices dry or stale bread

4 eggs

2 cups milk

1 cup raisins

1½ cups brown sugar

2 apples, cored, peeled, and chopped

1 very small onion, finely chopped

2 tablespoons cinnamon

1 teaspoon nutmeg

Shredded cheese and nuts (your favorite; optional)

1 cup (2 standard sticks) butter

"Capirotada is a bread pudding that was enjoyed by travelers along the Santa Fe Trail. Mountain men sometimes had trouble with the Spanish pronunciation, so they renamed the dish, calling it 'spotted dog' for the raisins in it. This recipe won first place in a local Scout-O-Rama cook-off."

PREPARATION AT CAMP:

1. Preheat Dutch oven over 25 coals.

2. Break bread into bite-size pieces and set aside.

3. In a medium-size bowl, beat eggs well then blend with milk.

4. To the eggs, add raisins, brown sugar, apples, onion, cinnamon, and nutmeg. Thoroughly mix. Add any optional ingredients at this time.

5. Melt butter in the Dutch oven then add bread pieces and egg mixture, blending well.

6. Bake for 25 to 35 minutes using 17 coals on the lid and 8 briquettes under the oven, until bread solidifies.

REQUIRED EQUIPMENT:
12-inch camp Dutch oven
Medium-size mixing bowl

David and Janet Stanger, Boise, Idaho
Committee Members
Venture Crew 60, Ore-Ida Council

Servings: 10–12
Preparation Time: 1¼ hours
Challenge Level: Easy

Dutch Oven Popcorn

PREPARATION AT CAMP:

1. Coat bottom of Dutch oven with oil then warm over 25 coals.

2. Cover bottom of oven with popcorn kernels. Replace lid.

3. Cook the corn, rotating oven ¼-turn per minute to avoid hot spots.

4. Remove oven from coals once corn popping begins to slow. Don't wait too long on this step; otherwise, popcorn will burn.

5. Carefully pour popcorn into a large serving bowl.

6. Add softened butter to the warm popcorn, if desired, then salt or season to taste.

REQUIRED EQUIPMENT:
12-inch camp Dutch oven
Large serving bowl

Tim Conners, Statesboro, Georgia
Assistant Scoutmaster
Troop 340, Coastal Empire Council

Christine Conners, Statesboro, Georgia
Committee Member and Merit Badge Counselor
Troop 340, Coastal Empire Council

¼ cup vegetable oil

¾ cup popcorn kernels

Salt and softened butter to taste

Options: Fun toppings include garlic salt, furikake, Cajun seasoning, Parmesan cheese, powdered sugar, onion powder, you name it.

Popcorn and a cup of coffee—that's civilized!
CHRISTINE CONNERS

Servings: 4
Preparation Time: ½ hour
Challenge Level: Moderate

Wrappin' Micro Pies

½ (12-ounce / 50-count) package medium-size wonton or gyoza wrappers

1½ cups jam or preserves, flavor of your choice

1 cup chopped walnuts

Ground cinnamon to taste

Ground nutmeg to taste

½ cup (1 standard stick) butter, melted

Canola oil for frying

Options: S'mores! Fill with chocolate chips, mini marshmallows, cinnamon, and nutmeg.

Peanut butter or mincemeat also make great dessert fillings.

"This recipe came to me as I was preparing for a Scout trip when, at the grocery store, I spotted premade wonton and gyoza wrappers used in Asian cooking. These wrappers are extremely versatile and fun to experiment with. Almost any filling can be used."

PREPARATION AT CAMP:

1. Place several wrappers on a flat surface and spoon about a tablespoon of jam or preserves onto half of each wrapper.

2. Sprinkle nuts, cinnamon, and nutmeg to taste over filling.

3. Dampen edge of wrapper and fold in half, sealing edge with a fork or fingers. Do not overfill the wrappers.

4. Flip the lid of the Dutch oven and support it on rocks or other heat-proof stand an inch or so over about 25 coals. Warm the lid.

5. Brush each wrapper with melted butter.

6. Heat oil in lid then fry wrapper pies until browned on each side.

REQUIRED EQUIPMENT:

12-inch camp Dutch oven

Curt "The Titanium Chef" White, Forks, Washington
Committee Member
Troop 1467, Chief Seattle Council

TIPS:
- Flipped over, the concave inside surface of a Dutch oven lid makes for a great substitute "wok." With coals concentrated to the center under the lid, the main frying can proceed from the hot center outward to the cooler perimeter.
- To double the cooking capacity and cut the total cooking time, the base of the Dutch oven can be used as a frying pan along with the lid.

Servings: 4–6
Preparation Time: ¾ hour
Challenge Level: Moderate

S'mores Cake

PREPARATION AT CAMP:

1. Slice pound cake lengthwise into 3 horizontal layers of approximately equal thickness.

2. Place the bottom layer of pound cake crosswise on a large sheet of aluminum foil.

3. Break up 3 chocolate bars and spread the pieces across the bottom layer of pound cake.

4. Layer half of the mini marshmallows over the chocolate.

5. Place the middle layer of pound cake on top of the marshmallows.

6. Repeat the chocolate and marshmallow layering.

7. Place the last layer of cake on top and wrap the entire stack securely in foil.

8. Place foil wrap in Dutch oven on trivet, and warm the cake for about 20 minutes using 20 coals on the lid and 10 briquettes under the oven, until the chocolate and marshmallows melt.

9. Remove from oven, carefully peel back the foil, slice, and serve.

REQUIRED EQUIPMENT:

14-inch camp Dutch oven with trivet
Heavy-duty aluminum foil (wide roll)

Katherine Osburn-Day, Ocala, Florida
Committee Member and Merit Badge Counselor
Troop 380, North Florida Council

1 (16-ounce) Sara Lee Pound Cake

6 (1½-ounce) chocolate bars

2 cups mini marshmallows

Option: Cake may also be warmed on the outer edge of a campfire or in the coals after cooking the entree.

Servings: 6–8
Preparation Time: ¾ hour
Challenge Level: Easy

5 cups fresh figs

1 tablespoon cornstarch

½ cup brown sugar

1 tablespoon lemon juice

2 (9-inch) deep-dish frozen piecrusts, thawed

Option: For a fancy shiny crust, brush the crust with a mixture of beaten eggs and a spoonful of water before baking.

TIPS:
- If the second crust is difficult to work with because it has thawed, the dough can be sliced into strips then laid in a traditional pie lattice over the fig mixture.
- If you can't find fresh figs, dried figs can be covered with water and chilled overnight to reconstitute. About 12 ounces of dried figs are required for this recipe.

Funky Fig Pie

"That's right, figs. You will love this recipe."

PREPARATION AT CAMP:

1. Remove stems from figs and cut each fig in half. Place fig pieces in a large bowl.

2. Add the cornstarch, brown sugar, and lemon juice to the bowl. Toss until all figs are coated.

3. Pour the fig mixture into one of the piecrusts, leaving the crust in the foil pan.

4. Carefully remove crust from the second pie pan and use it to top the fig mixture in the first pie crust.

5. Pinch together the edges of the first and second piecrusts and cut slits in the top crust to vent the steam.

6. Use the now-empty second pie pan as a trivet by placing it upside down in the bottom of the Dutch oven. Place the filled pie pan on top of the trivet.

7. Bake for 25 to 30 minutes, using 14 coals on the lid and 7 briquettes under the oven, until the crust is golden brown.

REQUIRED EQUIPMENT:

10-inch camp Dutch oven
Large mixing bowl

Mark Case, Randleman, North Carolina
Roundtable Commissioner
Troop 531, Old North State Council

Servings: 6–8
Preparation Time: 1 hour
Challenge Level: Easy

CPCC Pie

"When we bring new Scouts into our troop, we also like to reassure the new parents that adults seldom starve to death on camp cooking. I cook a 'show-off' dessert to drive home the point that we really do eat well on campouts. CPCC (coconut, pecan, and chocolate chip) Pie is one of my favorites for that."

PREPARATION AT CAMP:

1. Combine eggs, sugar, vinegar, and melted butter in a medium-size mixing bowl. Blend well.

2. Add coconut, pecans, and chocolate chips. Mix to combine, then pour batter into piecrust.

3. Place pie pan on trivet in Dutch oven and bake for 30 to 35 minutes using 16 coals on the lid and 7 briquettes under the oven, until the pie is firm and the top a golden brown.

4. Allow pie to cool before serving.

REQUIRED EQUIPMENT:
12-inch camp Dutch oven with trivet
Medium-size mixing bowl

Alan Ritter, St. Louis, Missouri
Eagle Scout and Committee Chairman
Troop 313, Greater St. Louis Area Council

3 eggs, lightly beaten

1½ cups granulated sugar

1½ tablespoons white vinegar

1 tablespoon butter, melted then cooled slightly

¾ cup flaked coconut

¾ cup chopped pecans

¾ cup dark chocolate chips

1 (9-inch) deep-dish or (10-inch) regular frozen piecrust, thawed

TIP:
If the pie hasn't finished baking after about 35 minutes, add a few more coals to the lid of the oven to finish cooking and to lightly brown the top of the pie.

Servings: 6–8
Preparation Time: 1 hour
Challenge Level: Easy

Frazzleberry Pie

2 (9-inch) deep-dish frozen piecrusts, thawed

2 cups blackberries, fresh, or frozen and thawed

2 cups raspberries, fresh, or frozen and thawed

2 tablespoons all-purpose flour

½ cup granulated sugar

½ cup brown sugar

1 teaspoon ground cinnamon

1 tablespoon butter

PREPARATION AT CAMP:

1. Preheat Dutch oven using 18 coals on the lid and 9 briquettes under the oven.

2. Gently remove piecrust from one pan and place that pan upside down in the oven to serve as a trivet. Set dough aside on a cutting tray.

3. Keep the second crust in its pan and place pan on the "trivet" in the oven.

4. Replace lid and bake second crust for about 10 minutes, until lightly browned.

5. While crust is cooking, combine berries, flour, sugars, and cinnamon in a medium-size mixing bowl.

6. Take the piecrust previously set aside and cut it into ¾-inch-wide strips. The pieces from the sides will be left over.

7. Once bottom crust is ready, remove from oven and pour berries into crust. Slice butter into four thin pats and place them evenly around the berry filling.

8. Lay strips of remaining crust dough in a latticework pattern over the top of the pie filling.

9. Return pie to the oven and bake for 20 to 30 minutes using 17 coals on the lid and 8 briquettes under the oven, until the lattice top is a golden brown. Refresh coals if required.

REQUIRED EQUIPMENT:

12-inch camp Dutch oven
Medium-size mixing bowl

David Visser, Hurst, Texas
Assistant Scoutmaster
Troop 340, Longhorn Council

Servings: 6–8
Preparation Time: 1¼ hours
Challenge Level: Easy

Log Cabin Snackin' Cake

"I bake this at Turkey Camp in a log cabin back in the hills of West Virginia every spring turkey season. The men like it so much, they make sure the shelves are stocked with tomato soup and chocolate cake mix when I get there."

1 (18½-ounce) package chocolate cake mix

1 (10½-ounce) can condensed tomato soup

¼ to ½ soup can water

Option: Use a 16-ounce package angel food cake mix in place of the chocolate cake mix, and a 20-ounce can crushed pineapple, including juice, in place of the tomato soup and water.

PREPARATION AT CAMP:

1. Coat inside of cake pan with vegetable oil.

2. Sift or stir the dry cake mix in a medium-size bowl to remove the lumps.

3. Add the condensed soup and as much water as needed to make a smooth batter.

4. Pour batter into cake pan then level the top of the batter so it will bake evenly.

5. Place cake pan on trivet in Dutch oven, and bake for 35 to 45 minutes, using 17 coals on the lid and 8 briquettes under the oven, until a toothpick comes out clean.

6. Remove snackin' cake from oven and allow to cool before slicing.

REQUIRED EQUIPMENT:

12-inch camp Dutch oven with trivet
8 x 8-inch or 9 x 9-inch cake pan
Medium-size mixing bowl

Ray McCune, Fort Wayne, Indiana
Committee Member
Troop 344, Anthony Wayne Area Council

Servings: 6–8
Preparation Time: 1½ hours
Challenge Level: Easy

10 tablespoons
(1¼ standard sticks)
butter, softened

¾ cup granulated sugar

¼ teaspoon salt

2 tablespoons honey, plus
a little extra for drizzle

4 eggs, lightly beaten

1 cup plus 2 tablespoons
all-purpose flour

1 pear, peeled, cored,
and diced

½ cup chopped walnuts

¼ cup whole walnut
pieces

TIP:
Nonna is Italian for
grandma or nana.

Nonna's Italian Walnut Cake

"I found this recipe in a copy of *La Cucina Italiana* cooking magazine several years ago and adapted it for the Dutch oven. It is easy, moist, and doesn't require a lot of ingredients. This recipe won second place in *Scouting* magazine's 2009 Great Tastes in Camp Cooking contest in the dessert category."

PREPARATION AT CAMP:

1. In a medium-size mixing bowl, cream together butter, sugar, and salt.

2. Add honey and eggs and blend well.

3. Gradually add the flour, mixing to combine.

4. Fold in diced pear and chopped walnuts.

5. Pour batter into greased Dutch oven and sprinkle with whole walnut pieces.

6. Bake for about 40 minutes using 13 coals on the lid and 6 briquettes under the oven, until a knife comes out clean.

7. Let the cake cool then drizzle with a little more honey.

REQUIRED EQUIPMENT:
10-inch camp Dutch oven
Medium-size mixing bowl

Beverly Jo Antonini, Morgantown, West Virginia
Assistant Scoutmaster
Troop 49, Mountaineer Area Council

Servings: 6–8
Preparation Time: 1½ hours
Challenge level: Easy

Grand Prize Lemon-Lime Apple Dumplings

"This recipe was the Grand Prize Winner of *Scouting* magazine's 2009 Great Tastes in Camp Cooking contest."

PREPARATION AT CAMP:

1. Wrap each piece of apple in one crescent roll, forming "dumplings."

2. Mix cinnamon with the sugar.

3. Warm the Dutch oven over 25 coals.

4. Melt the stick of butter in the bottom of Dutch oven and then roll each dumpling in the butter. Evenly distribute the dumplings over the bottom of the oven.

5. Sprinkle the cinnamon-sugar mix onto the dumplings.

6. Add the soda, but don't pour directly over the dumplings. You don't want to wash the sugar from them.

7. Bake for about 30 minutes using 17 coals on the lid and 8 briquettes under the oven, until the dumplings become a golden brown.

REQUIRED EQUIPMENT:

12-inch camp Dutch oven

Martin Pessink, Gladewater, Texas
Adviser
Crew 451, NeTseO Trails Council

2 large Granny Smith apples, cored, peeled, and cut into 8 pieces each

2 (8-ounce) containers refrigerated crescent rolls (8 rolls each)

1 tablespoon cinnamon (or more to taste)

1 cup granulated sugar

½ cup (1 standard stick) butter

1 (12-ounce) can lemon-lime soda

Option: These are great for dessert, but you can't beat them for breakfast on a cold morning.

Servings: 8 (2 dumplings each)
Preparation Time: 1¼ hours
Challenge Level: Easy

½ cup (1 standard stick) butter, softened

½ cup packed brown sugar

2 eggs, lightly beaten

1 cup chopped pecans

½ cup shredded coconut

1 cup mini marshmallows

½ cup semisweet chocolate morsels

1 teaspoon vanilla extract

½ cup all-purpose flour

1 standard-size ready-made graham cracker piecrust (such as Keebler Ready Crust)

Coconut S'mores Pie

"We have three sons in Troop 109 here in Rock Hill, and they love camping. My husband, Craig, is Assistant Scoutmaster for their troop, and he built a fire pit in our backyard, where we test new Dutch oven recipes before taking them 'on the road.' I invented this recipe because we all enjoy making s'mores, and this would be a new way to enjoy them."

PREPARATION AT CAMP:

1. Preheat Dutch oven using 17 coals on the lid and 8 briquettes under the oven.

2. Cream butter in a medium-size mixing bowl.

3. Add all remaining ingredients except the piecrust to bowl and mix thoroughly.

4. Pour batter mixture into piecrust.

5. Place pie pan on trivet in preheated Dutch oven and bake until top of pie becomes golden brown, about 30 to 40 minutes.

REQUIRED EQUIPMENT:

12-inch camp Dutch oven with trivet
Medium-size mixing bowl

Martha Charles, Rock Hill, South Carolina
Committee Member
Pack 161, Palmetto Council

Servings: 8–10
Preparation Time: 1 hour
Challenge Level: Easy

Old Colony Apple Crisp

"This one is from my mom to the woods. It serves 8 or more Scouts, but it's really too good to share."

PREPARATION AT CAMP:

1. Line Dutch oven with heavy-duty aluminum foil. Grease foil with a little of the butter.

2. Layer apple slices over foil and sprinkle with cinnamon.

3. In a medium-size bowl, blend sugar, flour, and oats with softened butter.

4. Cover apple slices in oven with the mixture.

5. Using 16 coals on the lid and 7 briquettes under the oven, bake for about 35 minutes, until apple crisp is golden brown on top.

REQUIRED EQUIPMENT:

12-inch camp Dutch oven
Medium-size mixing bowl
Heavy-duty aluminum foil

Andy Mills, Bridgewater, Massachusetts
Eagle Scout
Troop 4480, Old Colony Council

6–8 Granny Smith apples, peeled, cored, and sliced thin

1 tablespoon cinnamon

¾ cup brown sugar

½ cup all-purpose flour

¾ cup old-fashioned oats

½ cup (1 standard stick) butter, softened

Option: Goes great with a scoop of vanilla ice cream, provided the ice cream can be kept frozen in camp until serving time.

Servings: 8–10
Preparation Time: 1 hour
Challenge Level: Easy

Pineapple Casserole

3 eggs

1½ cups granulated sugar

¾ cup (1½ standard sticks) butter, melted

1 (20-ounce) can chunk pineapple (do not drain)

1 (8-count) package hot dog buns

Option: Reduce number of buns if a more moist dessert is preferred.

PREPARATION AT CAMP:

1. Beat eggs in medium-size bowl.

2. Blend sugar, melted butter, and pineapple juice with eggs.

3. Break buns into small pieces and spread over bottom of greased Dutch oven.

4. Gently mix pineapple chunks with bread pieces.

5. Pour egg mixture over bread-pineapple pieces and lightly stir.

6. Bake for 40 minutes, using 17 coals on the lid and 8 briquettes under the oven.

REQUIRED EQUIPMENT:
12-inch camp Dutch oven
Medium-size mixing bowl

Thomas Thibeault, Topsham, Maine
Adviser
Venture Crew 789, Pine Tree Council

TIP:
Small hamburger buns can be substituted for the hot dog buns.

Servings: 8–10
Preparation Time: 1 hour
Challenge Level: Easy

Patrol Stir-Crazy Cake

"Wow! Now this is campin'."

PREPARATION AT CAMP:

1. Grease inside of casserole pan.

2. In casserole pan, combine flour, 1½ cups sugar, cocoa powder, baking soda, and salt. Stir and make three "wells" in the flour mixture.

3. Into one well, pour the vegetable oil; into the second well, pour the vinegar; and into the third well, pour the vanilla extract.

4. Pour the Scoutmaster's cold leftover morning coffee over all the ingredients and stir until well mixed.

5. Combine remaining ¼ cup sugar and cinnamon in a cup and sprinkle over batter mixture.

6. Bake for 35 to 45 minutes, using 13 coals on the lid and 6 briquettes under the oven, until a fork inserted into the cake comes out clean.

7. Lift the foil pan from the Dutch oven and turn out onto a flat surface such as a large paper plate.

8. For the finishing touch, pour Hershey's Chocolate Syrup over the warm cake to taste, then serve.

REQUIRED EQUIPMENT:

10-inch camp Dutch oven
9¼-inch round x 2¾-inch deep aluminum foil casserole pan

Barry Moore, Auburndale, Florida
District Chairman
Lake Region District, Gulf Ridge Council

2½ cups all-purpose flour

1½ cups plus ¼ cup granulated sugar

½ cup cocoa powder

2 teaspoons baking soda

½ teaspoon salt

⅔ cup vegetable oil

2 tablespoons white vinegar

1 tablespoon vanilla extract

2 cups Scoutmaster's cold leftover morning coffee

½ teaspoon cinnamon

Hershey's Chocolate Syrup to taste

TIP:
Remove the cake from the foil pan by placing an inverted plate over the top of the cake then flipping both over so that the cake drops from the pan onto the plate.

Servings: 8–10
Preparation Time: 1¼ hours
Challenge Level: Easy

Gateau Chomage

CAKE:

3 tablespoons butter, softened

¾ cup granulated sugar

1½ cups all-purpose flour

2 teaspoons baking powder

1 teaspoon salt

¾ cup milk

SAUCE:

3 tablespoons butter

1 cup brown sugar

2 cups water

2 teaspoons vanilla extract

¼ cup all-purpose flour

Options: Use maple flavoring instead of vanilla. Add walnuts to the sauce mixture.

"*Gateau chomage* is French for unemployment cake. There are many different variations of this recipe that have been handed down from generation to generation throughout the Saint John Valley in Maine. This version is just as easy to make outdoors as it is indoors."

PREPARATION AT CAMP:

1. Preheat Dutch oven for a few minutes using 25 coals under the oven.

2. While oven warms, prepare the cake batter by creaming together 3 tablespoons butter and the granulated sugar in a medium-size mixing bowl.

3. Add 1½ cups flour, the baking powder, and salt to butter-sugar mix and blend well. Stir in the milk and set aside.

4. Prepare the sauce by melting butter in the warmed Dutch oven.

5. Add brown sugar, water, and vanilla extract to the oven. Mix then gradually stir in ¼ cup flour.

6. Drop cake batter, previously set aside, into sauce in the Dutch oven.

7. Bake for 30 to 40 minutes, using 17 coals on the lid and 8 briquettes under the oven, until a toothpick comes out clean. Refresh coals as necessary.

REQUIRED EQUIPMENT:
12-inch camp Dutch oven
Medium-size mixing bowl

David Guimond, Fort Kent, Maine
Committee Chair
Troop 189, Katahdin Area Council

Servings: 8–10
Preparation Time: 1¼ hours
Challenge Level: Easy

Mister Cannon's Peach Cobbler

"I started cooking cobblers at the age of 16 and tried many different recipes, from cake mixes to just about everything. When I made Eagle Scout some 32 years ago, I developed this recipe by reading a lot of my mother's notes that were in a handwritten cookbook. After several tries, this version worked, even winning first place at Camp Tayahua one year. I have created many other cobblers since, but my Scouts gave this recipe the name 'Mister Cannon's Cobbler,' and it just stuck over the years."

½ cup (1 standard stick) butter

2 cups granulated sugar

4 teaspoons baking soda

1½ cups all-purpose flour

2 pinches salt

1½ cups milk

1 (29-ounce) can peaches, drained

PREPARATION AT CAMP:

1. Melt the butter in Dutch oven over low heat. Remove oven from the coals or flame to keep butter from burning.

2. Combine the sugar, baking soda, flour, and salt in a large mixing bowl. Add milk and beat well.

3. Pour the cobbler batter over the butter in the oven.

4. Add peaches to the top of the batter mix. Do not stir. Bake for 50 to 60 minutes, using 17 coals on the lid and 8 briquettes under the oven, until a toothpick comes out clean. Refresh coals as necessary.

REQUIRED EQUIPMENT:
12-inch camp Dutch oven
Large mixing bowl

Glenn Cannon, Hubbard, Texas
Eagle Scout and Scoutmaster
Troop 404, Longhorn Council

Servings: 8–10
Preparation Time: 1½ hours
Challenge Level: Easy

Troop 27's Award-Winning Dutch Oven Ice Cream

1 (3.4-ounce) box instant pudding (any flavor)

1 cup milk

2 cups heavy cream

½ cup granulated sugar

½ tablespoon vanilla extract

¼ teaspoon lemon juice

1 (12-ounce) can evaporated milk

12–20 pounds crushed ice (depending on the size of tub)

2–3 cups rock salt (depending on the size of tub)

Water

Option: Top with your favorite fresh fruit or sundae fixings.

"When my troop prepared this for the Klondike Leader Dutch Oven Contest, I was careful to ask if the final product had to be made (as opposed to cooked) in a Dutch oven. I was told, 'Yes, made in a Dutch oven.' When the troop submitted the dish to the judges, they asked me, 'Where did the ice cream come from?' When I told them we had made it in a Dutch oven, they wanted to see proof. So I showed them pictures. My troop took first place!"

PREPARATION AT CAMP:

1. In a medium-size bowl, blend together pudding, milk, and 1 cup heavy cream.

2. In a second medium-size bowl, combine sugar, vanilla extract, and lemon juice.

3. To the second bowl, add evaporated milk and the remaining cup of heavy cream, then stir until smooth.

4. Combine the contents of the second bowl with the first bowl and mix well. Set aside.

5. Add about 2 inches of crushed ice to the bottom of a clean tub or cooler with the capacity to hold a Dutch oven.

6. Sprinkle about half of the rock salt over the ice. Set the Dutch oven on top of the ice.

7. Pack gap between oven and sides of tub with more crushed ice and the remainder of the rock salt. Keep the level of the ice and salt at least 1 to 2 inches below the rim of the Dutch oven to keep salt water from accidently sloshing into the ice cream.

8. Carefully pour water over the ice to the side of the Dutch oven to create a 2-inch-deep slurry at the bottom of the tub. Allow the oven to sit for about 10 minutes to chill.

Servings: 8–10

Preparation Time: 1¼ hours

Challenge Level: Moderate

9. Pour the ice cream mixture into the cold Dutch oven.

10. Add lid and cover completely with crushed ice. Do not put rock salt on the lid.

11. About 30 minutes after adding the lid to the oven, begin checking the ice cream every 10 minutes, stirring and scraping the mixture from the walls of the oven using a rubber spatula.

12. Once ice cream has solidified to a point where it is hard to stir, it is ready to serve. Total freezing time runs about 45 to 60 minutes.

REQUIRED EQUIPMENT:

12-inch camp Dutch oven
2 medium-size mixing bowls
Tub or cooler at least 18 inches wide

John Malachowski, Stewartstown, Pennsylvania
Scoutmaster
Troop 27, New Birth of Freedom Council

TIP:
The flavor of the pudding will become the final flavor of the ice cream.

Dutch oven ice cream! (Action figure sold separately.) *JOHN MALACHOWSKI*

Caramel Apple Pecan Pie

6 medium Granny Smith apples, cored, peeled, and sliced

1 tablespoon lemon juice

½ cup plus 3 tablespoons granulated sugar

2 tablespoons quick-cooking tapioca

¾ teaspoon ground cinnamon

¼ teaspoon salt

¼ teaspoon ground nutmeg

1 (9-inch) deep-dish frozen piecrust, thawed

¾ cup old-fashioned oats

1 tablespoon all-purpose flour

¼ cup (½ standard stick) butter

18 caramel candies

5 tablespoons milk

¼ cup pecans

PREPARATION AT CAMP:

1. In a medium-size bowl, combine apples and lemon juice.

2. In a small bowl, combine ½ cup sugar, tapioca, cinnamon, salt, and nutmeg.

3. Add contents of small bowl to apples. Stir gently, let stand for 15 minutes, then pour into piecrust.

4. Use small bowl to combine oats, flour, and remaining sugar. Cut in the butter until mixture is crumbly.

5. Sprinkle the oat mixture over the apples, and place the pie tin on the trivet in the oven.

6. Bake for 45 minutes using 17 coals on the lid and 8 briquettes under the oven. Refresh coals as required.

7. While the pie bakes, melt the caramels in milk using a small cook pot over low heat. Stir until smooth.

8. Add pecans to the caramel sauce then drizzle over pie.

9. Continue baking 8 to 10 minutes longer, until crust is golden brown and filling is bubbly.

10. Remove pie tin from oven and let cool on trivet before slicing and serving.

REQUIRED EQUIPMENT:

12-inch camp Dutch oven with trivet
Small cook pot
Medium-size mixing bowl
Small mixing bowl

Delano LaGow, Oswego, Illinois
Committee Member
Troop 31, Three Fires Council

Servings: 8–10
Preparation Time: 2 hours
Challenge Level: Moderate

Troop Chef's Monkey Bread

"My wife has made sticky buns in a bundt pan during the holidays for years. Then one year at summer camp, I had the idea to adapt her recipe for the Dutch oven. My son prepared it for a cooking competition because he was the one who always helped my wife make them at home. Well, he won first place for dessert; after that, he was appointed Troop Chef."

½ cup whole pecans

1 cup chopped pecans or walnuts

½ cup brown sugar

2 (3½-ounce) packages Jell-O Cook & Serve Butterscotch Pudding mix

1 teaspoon ground cinnamon

¾ cup (1½ standard sticks) butter, melted

2 (1-pound) loaves frozen bread dough, thawed

PREPARATION AT CAMP:

1. Pour the whole pecans into a well-greased Dutch oven.

2. Combine chopped nuts, brown sugar, pudding mix, and cinnamon in a medium-size bowl.

3. Sprinkle about one-third of the dry sugar-pudding mix into the oven and pour about a third of the melted butter over the mix.

4. Cut or tear the bread dough into small 1-inch pieces and layer in oven.

5. Top dough with another third of the dry mix and one-third of the butter.

6. Cut up the second bread loaf and layer it like the first.

7. Pour the remainder of the dry mix and butter over the dough.

8. Cook for 35 to 45 minutes using 16 coals on the lid and 9 briquettes under the oven.

9. Cut around the sides of the bread to loosen, then carefully invert the oven to drop the monkey bread onto a serving tray.

REQUIRED EQUIPMENT:
12-inch camp Dutch oven
Medium-size mixing bowl

Tim Yezzi, Erie, Pennsylvania
Committee Member
Troop 96, French Creek Council

Servings: 10–12
Preparation Time: 1 hour
Challenge Level: Easy

Little Jimmycamper's Strawberry Shortcake

2 cups mini marshmallows

6 cups fresh strawberries, sliced

1 (3-ounce) package strawberry gelatin mix

1 (18½-ounce) package Pillsbury yellow cake mix

1 cup water

⅓ cup oil

3 eggs

Whipped cream (optional)

PREPARATION AT CAMP:

1. Spread marshmallows evenly over bottom of greased Dutch oven.

2. In a small bowl, combine strawberries and gelatin mix. Set aside.

3. In a large bowl, blend the cake mix with the water, oil, and eggs.

4. Pour cake batter evenly over the marshmallows, then spoon the strawberry mixture over the batter.

5. Bake for 45 to 55 minutes, using 17 coals on the lid and 8 briquettes under the oven, until the top is a golden brown. Refresh coals as necessary.

6. Top with optional whipped cream and serve.

REQUIRED EQUIPMENT:

12-inch camp Dutch oven
Small mixing bowl
Large mixing bowl

Jim "Little Jimmycamper" Landis, New Providence, Pennsylvania
Unit Commissioner
Conestoga River District, Pennsylvania Dutch Council

Servings: 10–12
Preparation Time: 1¼ hours
Challenge Level: Easy

Backwoods Brownies

PREPARATION AT CAMP:

1. In a medium-size bowl, prepare batter by combining 1⅔ cups granulated sugar, ¾ cup butter, water, eggs, and 2 teaspoons vanilla extract.

2. Mix flour, ¾ cup cocoa powder, baking powder, and salt in a second medium-size bowl.

3. Blend flour-cocoa mixture into sugar mixture. Add nuts and stir.

4. Spread brownie batter into greased Dutch oven.

5. Bake for 30 to 40 minutes using 17 coals on the lid and 8 briquettes under the oven.

6. While the brownies bake, prepare the frosting by combining all the frosting ingredients in one of the medium-size bowls. Beat until creamy.

7. After brownies have baked and cooled, cover with frosting and serve.

REQUIRED EQUIPMENT:

12-inch camp Dutch oven
2 medium-size mixing bowls

Tim Conners, Statesboro, Georgia
Assistant Scoutmaster
Troop 340, Coastal Empire Council

Christine Conners, Statesboro, Georgia
Committee Member and Merit Badge Counselor
Troop 340, Coastal Empire Council

BROWNIE BATTER:
1⅔ cups granulated sugar

¾ cup (1½ standard sticks) butter, melted

2 tablespoons water

2 large eggs

2 teaspoons vanilla extract

1⅓ cups all-purpose flour

¾ cup cocoa powder

½ teaspoon baking powder

¼ teaspoon salt

1 cup chopped nuts

FROSTING:
3 cups confectioners' sugar

⅔ cup cocoa powder

½ cup (1 standard stick) butter, softened

⅓ cup milk

1 teaspoon vanilla extract

Servings: 10–12
Preparation Time: 1½ hours
Challenge Level: Easy

Snow Buck Pumpkin Spice Cake

1 (15-ounce) can pure pumpkin (not pumpkin pie mix)

2 (18¼-ounce) packages spice cake mix (any brand)

Butter to grease pan

1 cup confectioners' sugar

2 tablespoons water

"I once had a mother approach me at a meeting to tell me that her son, a Scout in my troop, had lied to her about baking a cake while camping. 'Everyone knows you can't bake a cake on a campout,' she said. So I had her son take a Dutch oven home and show his mother that he could indeed bake outdoors. She apologized later: 'He didn't even know how to boil water before.' I think I helped to make one mother proud."

PREPARATION AT CAMP:

1. Preheat Dutch oven with 21 coals on the lid and 11 briquettes under the oven.

2. Thoroughly blend pumpkin with the spice cake mix in a large bowl.

3. Pour batter into greased angel food cake pan and place on trivet in oven.

4. Bake for 1 hour and 15 minutes, refreshing coals as needed.

5. Remove cake and let cool for about 5 minutes. Turn cake upside down over a cooling rack or tray, twisting pan to remove cake. Allow cake to cool completely.

6. Knead confectioners' sugar with water in a small ziplock bag to create icing.

7. Snip a small corner from the bag. Squeeze, drizzling icing over the cooled cake.

REQUIRED EQUIPMENT:

Deep 14-inch camp Dutch oven with trivet
Large mixing bowl
Angel food cake pan
Small ziplock bag

Ray McCune, Fort Wayne, Indiana
Committee Member
Troop 344, Anthony Wayne Area Council

Servings: 10–12
Preparation Time: 2 hours
Challenge Level: Easy

Kybo Pudding

PREPARATION AT CAMP:

1. Fill bottom of Dutch oven with doughnuts.

2. Cover doughnuts with chocolate pieces and sprinkle with cinnamon.

3. Pour maple syrup and milk over all.

4. Bake for 30 to 40 minutes, using 17 coals on the lid and 8 briquettes under the oven.

REQUIRED EQUIPMENT:

12-inch camp Dutch oven

William Souza, Puyallup, Washington
Assistant Scoutmaster
Troop 598, Pacific Harbors Council

2 (16-ounce) packages mini cinnamon-sugar dusted cake doughnuts

2 (2.6-ounce) Hershey's chocolate bars, broken into pieces

2 teaspoons ground cinnamon

12 ounces maple syrup

3 cups whole milk

Another dessert masterpiece. SCOTT H. SIMERLY SR.

Servings: 12–14
Preparation Time: 1 hour
Challenge Level: Easy

Jayhawk Apple Cobbler

8 Granny Smith apples, peeled, cored, and thinly sliced

1 cup brown sugar

1 (6-ounce) package Sugar Babies candy

1 (12-ounce) can Sprite soda

1 (16-ounce) package angel food cake mix

½ cup (1 standard stick) butter, sliced into pats

1 tablespoon ground cinnamon

PREPARATION AT CAMP:

1. Place apple slices in the Dutch oven and cover with brown sugar.

2. Layer Sugar Babies over the brown sugar. Pour Sprite over all.

3. Cover with dry angel food cake mix.

4. Layer slices of butter over cake mix and sprinkle cinnamon on top.

5. Bake for 30 to 40 minutes, using 17 coals on the lid and 8 briquettes under the oven, until the liquid is bubbling and the top becomes golden brown.

REQUIRED EQUIPMENT:

12-inch camp Dutch oven

Keith Shaver, Emporia, Kansas
Assistant Scoutmaster
Troop 157, Jayhawk Area Council

Servings: 12–14
Preparation Time: 1 hour
Challenge Level: Easy

Calusa Double-Chocolate Cake

"This recipe won the Dutch oven cooking contest at our annual Calusa District Rendezvous. The original recipe called for a cake mix. But I wanted to make it a little more difficult for the boys because I felt they had acquired the skill necessary to prepare it completely from scratch."

PREPARATION AT CAMP:

1. Combine flour, sugar, cocoa powder, baking soda, salt, and buttermilk powder in a large mixing bowl.

2. Add oil, sour cream, and eggs, then blend well.

3. Stir in pudding mix and chocolate chips.

4. Line the Dutch oven with foil, grease the foil, then pour batter into the oven.

5. Bake for about 45 minutes using 17 coals on the lid and 8 coals under the oven, until a knife comes out clean. Refresh coals as needed.

6. Cool the cake slightly then sprinkle with confectioners' sugar before serving.

REQUIRED EQUIPMENT:

12-inch camp Dutch oven
Large mixing bowl

Donna Cochran, Sebring, Florida
Committee Chair
Troop 808, Gulf Ridge Council

1⅔ cups all-purpose flour

1½ cups granulated sugar

⅔ cup cocoa powder

1½ teaspoons baking soda

1 teaspoon salt

3 tablespoons buttermilk powder

¾ cup vegetable oil

2 cups sour cream

4 eggs

1 (3.9-ounce) package instant chocolate pudding mix

1 (12-ounce) bag chocolate chips

¼ cup confectioners' sugar

Option: Goes great with ice cream.

TIP:
The dry ingredients can be mixed at home before leaving for camp.

Servings: 12–14
Preparation Time: 1½ hours
Challenge Level: Easy

Apple Caramel Dump Cake (aka Boston Baked Beans)

3 (20-ounce) cans regular apple pie filling

½ teaspoon ground cinnamon

1 (18½-ounce) package Duncan Hines Spice Cake mix

½ cup brown sugar

¼ cup (½ standard stick) butter, sliced into pats

1 (14-ounce) bag Kraft caramels

"A couple of years ago at summer camp, another Scouter was helping me in the annual Scoutmaster Dutch oven competition. I had found a new kind of caramel candy that came in little balls, which I thought would melt easier than the cubes. I asked my partner to add the caramels, which he did, using the entire bag and covering all the filling. A little while later, I lifted the lid to check progress and saw that the now partially melted caramel balls made the recipe look like a pot of Boston baked beans. I was busy at the competition, and the volunteers placing the entries in the proper categories also thought they saw beans when they popped the lid. It was all straightened out at judging time when our Apple Caramel Dump Cake went missing, and I found it in the vegetables area. We ended up with first place in desserts and got an honorable mention in veggies."

PREPARATION AT CAMP:

1. Pour apple pie filling into foil-lined Dutch oven. Sprinkle with cinnamon.

2. In a medium-size bowl, combine dry spice cake mix with brown sugar then spread over the apple pie filling in the oven.

3. Lay pats of butter evenly over the cake mix. Place caramel cubes over top.

4. Bake for 50 minutes to 1 hour, using 17 coals on the lid and 8 briquettes under the oven.

REQUIRED EQUIPMENT:
12-inch camp Dutch oven
Medium-size mixing bowl
Heavy-duty aluminum foil

Ray Sigmon, Randleman, North Carolina
Scoutmaster
Troop 531, Old North State Council

Servings: 16–18
Preparation Time: 1¼ hours
Challenge Level: Easy

Camp Maumee Chipotle Apple Spice Cake

"My son, Nathan, an Eagle Scout, took first place in the dessert category with this recipe at a camporee cook-off at Camp Maumee."

PREPARATION AT CAMP:

1. Lightly coat the inside of the Dutch oven with cooking spray or vegetable oil, and sprinkle with a little flour.

2. In a large bowl, combine remainder of flour, cinnamon, nutmeg, baking soda, chipotle pepper, ginger, white pepper, salt, and cloves. Set aside.

3. In a medium-size mixing bowl, beat the oil, sugar, and vanilla extract.

4. Add eggs to the sugar-oil mixture, blending them one at a time.

5. Add the sugar-oil-egg mixture to the flour mix previously set aside. Combine with the apples and pecans then mix well. Pour batter into the Dutch oven.

6. Bake for 1 to 1¼ hours, using 17 coals on the lid and 8 briquettes under the oven, until wooden toothpick comes out clean. Refresh coals as required.

7. While cake is baking, prepare the spicy caramel glaze by combining brown sugar, butter, whipping cream, and chipotle pepper in a small cook pot.

8. Bring glaze mixture to a low boil for 2 minutes while stirring gently.

9. Remove glaze from heat, then blend in vanilla extract.

10. Once cake has finished baking and has cooled, reheat the glaze, if required to liquefy, then drizzle the glaze over the cake.

REQUIRED EQUIPMENT:

12-inch camp Dutch oven
Small cook pot
Large mixing bowl
Medium-size mixing bowl

Mike Noll, Columbus, Indiana
Scoutmaster
Troop 555, Hoosier Trails Council

CAKE:
3 cups all-purpose flour

2 teaspoons cinnamon

1½ teaspoons nutmeg

1 teaspoon baking soda

1 teaspoon ground chipotle pepper

¾ teaspoon ground ginger

½ teaspoon ground white pepper

¼ teaspoon salt

⅛ teaspoon ground cloves

1½ cups vegetable oil

1¾ cups granulated sugar

1 tablespoon vanilla extract

3 eggs

3 large tart apples, peeled, cored, and diced

1 cup chopped toasted pecans

SPICY CARAMEL GLAZE:
½ cup packed brown sugar

¼ cup (½ standard stick) butter

¼ cup whipping cream

½ teaspoon ground chipotle pepper

1 teaspoon vanilla extract

Servings: 16–18
Preparation Time: 2 hours
Challenge Level: Moderate

CRUST:
⅔ package (2 sealed packets, about 10 ounces) graham crackers, crushed

½ cup brown sugar

½ cup granulated sugar

½ cup (1 standard stick) butter, melted

FILLING:
3 (8-ounce) packages reduced-fat cream cheese, softened

3 eggs

1 cup granulated sugar

1 tablespoon key lime juice (from about 2 key limes)

1 cup all-purpose flour

1 (14-ounce) can sweetened condensed milk

½ cup mango puree

1½ cups fresh thinly sliced mango

1 (7-ounce) can whipped cream (optional)

TIP:
Ataulfo mangos work well for the garnish, but any type is tasty.

Servings: 18–20
Preparation Time: 1¼ hour
Challenge Level: Moderate

Roundtable Mango Cheesecake

"I usually bring cheesecakes to Roundtable, where I was challenged a few years ago to make one in the Dutch oven. Some told me it couldn't be done. Not only did I prove the naysayers wrong, but I have been preparing a variety of Dutch oven cheesecakes ever since. This recipe has been one of the most popular."

PREPARATION AT CAMP:

1. To prepare crust, combine crushed graham crackers, brown sugar, ½ cup granulated sugar, and the melted butter in a medium-size bowl. Mix until the butter is absorbed and the crumbs are uniformly moist.

2. Line Dutch oven with heavy-duty aluminum foil, and evenly press crumb mixture into bottom and up sides of oven to form crust.

3. Add all filling ingredients to a large mixing bowl and blend using a hand mixer. Pour filling over crust in Dutch oven.

4. Using 16 coals on the lid and 7 briquettes under the oven, bake for about 45 minutes, until top of cheesecake begins to brown. When it is finished baking, the cake should still have a small wobbly area in the center. Do not overcook.

5. Remove Dutch oven from coals and top cheesecake with mango slices. Serve warm with optional whipped cream topping.

REQUIRED EQUIPMENT:
12-inch camp Dutch oven
Medium-size mixing bowl
Large mixing bowl
Heavy-duty aluminum foil
Hand mixer

Mark Case, Randleman, North Carolina
Roundtable Commissioner
Troop 531, Old North State Council

Black Forest Ribbon Cake

"This is one of our troop's favorite desserts. It won second place in a Cub Scout Fun-n-Sun event a few years back."

PREPARATION AT CAMP:

1. Combine cream cheese, 1 egg, and sugar in medium-size bowl and blend until smooth.

2. Gradually add milk, butter, cornstarch, and vanilla extract to the cream cheese mix, beating well. Set aside.

3. In a large mixing bowl, combine the package of brownie mix with 2 eggs, water, and vegetable oil (as directed on package).

4. Line Dutch oven with aluminum foil, and grease the foil.

5. Spread half of brownie batter into Dutch oven.

6. Spoon cream cheese mixture evenly over the batter.

7. Finally top with the remaining brownie batter.

8. Bake for an hour, using 17 coals on the lid and 8 briquettes under the oven, until a toothpick comes out clean. Refresh coals as necessary.

9. Let cool, then smooth frosting over cake and top with cherry filling.

REQUIRED EQUIPMENT:

12-inch camp Dutch oven
Medium-size mixing bowl
Large mixing bowl
Heavy-duty aluminum foil

Ingrid Oosthuizen, Lampasas, Texas
Assistant Scoutmaster
Troop 200, Texas Trails Council

1 (8-ounce) package cream cheese, softened

3 large eggs

¼ cup granulated sugar

3 tablespoons milk

2 tablespoons butter, softened

1 tablespoon cornstarch

1 teaspoon vanilla extract

1 (19.9-ounce) package Duncan Hines Chewy Fudge brownie mix

¼ cup water

½ cup vegetable oil

1 (16-ounce) can chocolate fudge frosting

2 (21-ounce) cans cherry pie filling

Servings: 18–20
Preparation Time: 2 hours
Challenge Level: Moderate

143

Three Rivers Pineapple-Orange Surprise Cobbler

1 cup (2 standard sticks) butter, sliced into pats

2 (18¼-ounce) packages Duncan Hines Orange Supreme cake mix

2 cups sugar

2 (20-ounce) cans crushed pineapple, with juice

2 (15-ounce) cans mandarin orange segments, with half of juice reserved

1 (6-ounce) package Ferrera Pan Red Hots candy

1 (8-ounce) can sliced pineapple, drained

1 (10-ounce) jar maraschino cherries

"Since its creation, I have entered this recipe into five Scoutmaster cobbler competitions over the years and took first place each time."

PREPARATION AT CAMP:

1. Line Dutch oven with foil then preheat for about 10 minutes with 21 coals on the lid and 11 briquettes under the oven.

2. Remove lid and carefully place about a quarter of the butter pats in the bottom of the hot oven.

3. Evenly distribute 1 package of dry cake mix on top of butter.

4. Sprinkle 1 cup of sugar over cake mix then pour 1 can crushed pineapple over sugar.

5. On top of this, spread orange segments from 1 can along with half of its juice (discard remainder of juice).

6. Sprinkle half of Red Hots over the top.

7. Spread half of butter pats over all.

8. Repeat layering of ingredients in steps 3 through 6, reserving a little of the sugar.

9. Distribute remaining butter pats on top followed by the pineapple rings.

10. Place a cherry in the middle of each pineapple ring and around the edges. Sprinkle the remaining sugar over all.

11. Return lid to the oven and bake for about 1½ hours, until a knife comes out clean. Refresh coals as necessary.

REQUIRED EQUIPMENT:
Deep 14-inch camp Dutch oven
Heavy-duty aluminum foil

Tony May, Dayton, Texas
Scoutmaster and Venture Crew Adviser
Troop and Crew 64, Three Rivers Council

Servings: 18–20
Preparation Time: 2¼ hours
Challenge Level: Easy

Rocky Road Freedom Fudge

"This recipe can be prepared using standard cook pots, but was adapted for a Dutch oven because the Camporee contest rules stated that it had to be prepared in a Dutch oven. It won the contest!"

PREPARATION AT CAMP:

1. Over 25 coals, heat 1 quart of water in the Dutch oven to simmering. Reduce coal count if boil becomes vigorous.

2. While the water heats, line the cake pan with aluminum foil then grease the foil.

3. In the metal mixing bowl, combine baking chocolates, baking soda, salt, and half the chocolate chips.

4. Slowly add the sweetened condensed milk and the vanilla extract, stirring everything together.

5. Place the metal bowl in the Dutch oven and stir with a rubber spatula until the chocolate is melted. Note that the oven is serving as a "double-boiler." The metal bowl should "float" in the hot water while the chocolate melts.

6. Remove bowl from the Dutch oven and continue stirring for an additional minute.

7. Add mini marshmallows, chopped pecans, and remaining chocolate chips to the bowl. Stir briefly.

8. Pour fudge into cake pan and evenly spread with spatula.

9. Lightly score the fudge into squares, 1 inch on a side.

10. Place cake pan on ice in a cooler and chill for about 2 hours or until the fudge is firm.

11. Remove fudge from the pan and peel foil from the sides and bottom. Cut fudge into 1-inch squares.

REQUIRED EQUIPMENT:
12-inch camp Dutch oven
8 x 8-inch cake pan
Medium-size metal mixing bowl
Heavy-duty aluminum foil
Rubber spatula

John Malachowski, Stewartstown, Pennsylvania
Scoutmaster
Troop 27, New Birth of Freedom Council

1 quart water

1 pound semisweet baking chocolate squares, chopped

2 ounces unsweetened baking chocolate squares, chopped

½ teaspoon baking soda

⅛ teaspoon salt

¼ cup semisweet chocolate chips, divided

1 (14-ounce) can sweetened condensed milk

2 tablespoons vanilla extract

1 cup mini marshmallows

1 cup pecans, chopped

Servings: 64 1-inch square pieces (about 2½ pounds of fudge)
Preparation Time: 2¾ hours
Challenge Level: Moderate

Appendix A

COMMON MEASUREMENT CONVERSIONS

United States Volumetric Conversions

1 smidgen	$\frac{1}{32}$ teaspoon
1 pinch	$\frac{1}{16}$ teaspoon
1 dash	$\frac{1}{8}$ teaspoon
3 teaspoons	1 tablespoon
48 teaspoons	1 cup
2 tablespoons	$\frac{1}{8}$ cup
4 tablespoons	$\frac{1}{4}$ cup
5 tablespoons + 1 teaspoon	$\frac{1}{3}$ cup
8 tablespoons	$\frac{1}{2}$ cup
12 tablespoons	$\frac{3}{4}$ cup
16 tablespoons	1 cup
1 ounce	2 tablespoons
4 ounces	$\frac{1}{2}$ cup
8 ounces	1 cup
$\frac{5}{8}$ cup	$\frac{1}{2}$ cup + 2 tablespoons
$\frac{7}{8}$ cup	$\frac{3}{4}$ cup + 2 tablespoons
2 cups	1 pint
2 pints	1 quart
1 quart	4 cups
4 quarts	1 gallon
1 gallon	128 ounces

Note: Dry and fluid volumes are equivalent for teaspoon, tablespoon, and cup.

International Metric System Conversions

Volume and Weight

United States	Metric
¼ teaspoon	1.25 milliliters
½ teaspoon	2.50 milliliters
¾ teaspoon	3.75 milliliters
1 teaspoon	5 milliliters
1 tablespoon	15 milliliters
1 ounce (volume)	30 milliliters
¼ cup	60 milliliters
½ cup	120 milliliters
¾ cup	180 milliliters
1 cup	240 milliliters
1 pint	0.48 liter
1 quart	0.95 liter
1 gallon	3.79 liters
1 ounce (weight)	28 grams
1 pound	0.45 kilogram

Temperature

Degrees F	Degrees C
175	80
200	95
225	105
250	120
275	135
300	150
325	165
350	175
375	190
400	205
425	220
450	230
475	245
500	260

British, Canadian, and Australian Conversions

1 teaspoon (Britain, Canada, Australia). . approx. 1 teaspoon (United States)

1 tablespoon (Britain, Canada). . . . . . . approx. 1 tablespoon (United States)

1 tablespoon (Australia) . . . . 1.35 tablespoons (United States)

1 ounce (Britain, Canada, Australia). . . . 0.96 ounce (United States)

1 gill (Britain) . . . . 5 ounces (Britain, Canada, Australia)

1 cup (Britain). . . . . 10 ounces (Britain, Canada, Australia)

1 cup (Britain). . . . . 9.61 ounces (United States)

1 cup (Britain). . . . . 1.20 cups (United States)

1 cup (Canada, Australia) . . . . 8.45 ounces (United States)

1 cup (Canada, Australia) . . . . 1.06 cups (United States)

1 pint (Britain, Canada, Australia). . . . . 20 ounces (Britain, Canada, Australia)

1 Imperial gallon (Britain). . . . . 1.20 gallons (United States)

1 pound (Britain, Canada, Australia) . . . 1 pound (United States)

Equivalent Measures*

16 ounces water . . . . 1 pound

2 cups vegetable oil . . . . 1 pound

2 cups or 4 sticks butter. . . . . 1 pound

2 cups granulated sugar. . . . . 1 pound

3½ to 4 cups unsifted confectioners' sugar . . . . 1 pound

2¼ cups packed brown sugar . . . . 1 pound

4 cups sifted flour . . . . 1 pound

3½ cups unsifted whole wheat flour . . . . 1 pound

8–10 egg whites. . . . . 1 cup

12–14 egg yolks. . . . . 1 cup

1 whole lemon, squeezed . . . . 3 tablespoons juice

1 whole orange, squeezed. . . . . ⅓ cup juice

* Approximate

Appendix B

SOURCES OF EQUIPMENT

Bass Pro Shops
www.basspro.com
Bass Pro stocks a large line of gear perfect for car camping, including a wide array of Lodge Dutch ovens and accessories. Bass Pro stores are a good place to go to see the equipment first-hand before you buy.

Boy Scout Catalog
www.scoutstuff.org
BSA Supply carries an assortment of handy camp kitchen gear as well as Lodge camp Dutch ovens in a range of sizes.

Cabela's
www.cabelas.com
This retailer specializes as a hunting and fishing outfitter but also carries a wide selection of outdoor kitchen gear and cookware. Cabela's has dozens of large retail stores located throughout the United States and Southern Canada.

Camp Chef
www.campchef.com
Many camp Dutch oven accessories are available through Camp Chef. The company also markets their own line of aluminum and cast-iron Dutch ovens.

Campmor
www.campmor.com

You won't find a large line of camp Dutch ovens or accessories at Campmor. However, Campmor does carry a huge selection of general camping supplies, many of them valuable for rounding out your list of basic equipment for a remotely located camp kitchen, farther from the car, where lightweight and compact become important characteristics for your gear.

Chuck Wagon Supply

www.chuckwagonsupply.com

The range of Dutch ovens and accessories at Chuck Wagon is truly impressive. This is a great site to compare different oven makes and models and to discover all those items that you didn't know you needed. If you are looking for the lighter weight of aluminum ovens, you'll find a nice selection here.

Dutch Oven Gear

www.dutchovengear.com

Scouter Sami Dahdal is CEO of Sam's Iron Works and its sister company, Dutch Oven Gear. A master wrought iron craftsman, Sam manufactures quality tables and accessories for camp Dutch ovens. Stop by the website to see his gear in action.

Lodge Manufacturing

www.lodgemfg.com

Founded in 1896, Lodge is the premier source of a large array of high-quality cast-iron cookware and related accessories. It is the only company that still manufactures its full line of camp cast-iron cookware in the United States.

MACA Supply

www.macaovens.com

MACA manufacturers a wide range of very deep camp cast-iron Dutch ovens, including what must be the largest on the market: a monster sporting a lid 22 inches in diameter and weighing in at 160 pounds. MACA also makes oval-shaped ovens, useful for roasting birds and larger cuts of meat.

REI

www.rei.com

Like Campmor, REI carries a large array of gear useful for the remote camp kitchen. REI also stocks a wide assortment of Dutch ovens and accessories by Lodge.

Sport Chalet

www.sportchalet.com

Sport Chalet is a major outdoor recreation retailer in the southwest United States. Like Bass Pro Shops, this is a good place to go to see camp kitchen gear, Lodge camp Dutch ovens, and related accessories before making the purchase.

Stack of Dutch ovens, 16-inch diameter at bottom, deep 14-inch above it, 12-inch second from top, and 10-inch at top. These four ovens were used to prepare every recipe in this book. TIM CONNERS

Appendix C

ADDITIONAL READING AND RESOURCES

Books and Periodicals

Chuck Wagon Supply Bookstore

www.chuckwagonsupply.com

This Dutch oven specialty shop has a great selection of books specific to the topic. The company also posts a wealth of helpful information for those new to Dutch oven cooking.

Cook's Illustrated and *Cook's Country*

www.cooksillustrated.com and www.cookscountry.com

These outstanding periodicals from America's Test Kitchen turn common recipes into wonderful re-creations but with a minimum amount of effort. Along the way, the reader learns how and why the recipes work. *Cook's Illustrated* explores fewer dishes but in more detail than *Cook's Country*, its sister publication, which comes in a larger format and full color. These are magazines for the home kitchen. But what you'll learn indoors will prove invaluable at camp.

Cooking, Merit Badge Series, Boy Scouts of America

Scouts interested in Dutch oven cooking will naturally want to pursue the Cooking Merit Badge on their way to Eagle. This booklet covers the basics of indoor and outdoor cooking, food safety and nutrition, and careers in the food service industry. Detailed Cooking Merit Badge requirements are included.

Lodge Manufacturing Bookstore

www.lodgemfg.com

Lodge is the preeminent manufacturer of camp Dutch oven cookware. At Lodge factory outlet stores and on their website, you'll find a wide range of books and DVDs focusing on camp Dutch oven recipes and cooking techniques.

***On Food and Cooking: The Science and Lore of the Kitchen,*
Harold McGee, Scribner**

This is an excellent resource for understanding the science behind cooking. When chefs decipher why recipes work the way they do, they become much more effective at adapting recipes in a pinch or creating new ones on the fly. Be forewarned. This is not a cookbook, much less an outdoor cookbook. But if science interests you, this book will too.

***The Scout's Outdoor Cookbook,* Tim and Christine Conners,
Globe Pequot Press**

The founding title of the Scout's Cookbook series, this book puts more emphasis on recipes and less on technique. All popular forms of camp cooking are represented, with Dutch oven recipes dominating. Over 300 recipes are included, many award-winning, and all provided by Scout leaders from across the United States.

***The Scout's Large Groups Cookbook,* Tim and Christine Conners, Globe Pequot Press**

Focusing on the art of cooking for groups larger than the typical Patrol, this book delves into technique without skimping on the recipes. Dozens of outdoor cooking experts from throughout Boy Scouts of America contributed over 100 outstanding and unique camp recipes for 10 to 20 people or more, many of the recipes designed for the Dutch oven.

For more recipes and information on outdoor cooking, an online search using the tag "camp Dutch oven cookbook" will reveal a wealth of other sources.

Informational Websites

Epicurious

www.epicurious.com

You won't find much on Dutch oven cooking at Epicurious. But if you're looking to hone your basic cooking skills and could use thousands of recipes for practice, this is a good resource.

Exploratorium

www.exploratorium.edu/cooking

Exploratorium makes cooking fun by putting emphasis on the science behind it. Even if you're not the scientist type, you'll enjoy this site. Quirky yet practical, recipes flow down the page with relevant science posted in the sidebar.

Gourmet Sleuth

www.gourmetsleuth.com

A good kitchen measurement conversion calculator can be found at this website. Included is the ability to convert between United States and British measurement units.

International Dutch Oven Society (IDOS)

www.idos.com

The mission of IDOS is to preserve the art of Dutch oven cooking. According to IDOS, they are the largest and most productive group of "black pot" enthusiasts in the world. This is the organization to join once you're smitten by the camp Dutch oven bug.

Leave No Trace (LNT) Center for Outdoor Ethics

www.LNT.org

The Center for Outdoor Ethics has been a leader and respected voice in communicating why and how our outdoor places require responsible stewardship. The LNT outdoor ethics code is becoming standard practice within Scouting. More information about the organization is available at their website, and specific information about outdoor ethics principles, especially as applied to cooking, can be found in Appendix D of this book.

Appendix D

LOW-IMPACT COOKING

"Leave a place better than you found it." A Scout hears that phrase innumerable times over the years. In fact, low-impact wilderness ethics has become a core principle within Scouting, the mastery of which is a requirement for rank advancement.

Early Scoutcraft emphasized skills for adapting the camp environment to suit the needs of the outdoorsman. But in more recent years, with increasing use and pressure on our wild places, the emphasis has rightfully shifted toward developing wilderness skills within the context of minimizing one's impact on the outdoors and others.

In fact, the Boy Scout Outdoor Code states:

> *As an American, I will do my best to*
> *Be clean in my outdoor manners*
> *Be careful with fire*
> *Be considerate in the outdoors*
> *Be conservation-minded*

By conscientiously following the Scout Outdoor Code, we become better and more thoughtful stewards of our natural resources.

The Leave No Trace Center for Outdoor Ethics also provides a set of principles that are becoming increasingly well known and applied within Scouting. These align closely with the Scout Outdoor Code. The principles of outdoor ethics from Leave No Trace enhance those of the Scout Outdoor Code by providing additional detail on their application.

The seven core principles of Leave No Trace are:

1. Plan ahead and prepare

2. Travel and camp on durable surfaces

3. Dispose of waste properly

4. Leave what you find

5. Minimize campfire impacts

6. Respect wildlife

7. Be considerate of other visitors

Careful planning, especially with respect to food preparation, is critical to successfully following the principles of both the Scout Outdoor Code and Leave No Trace, all of which are touched on once at camp. When preparing for an upcoming outing, consider the following list of application points as you discuss food and cooking options with your fellow Scouts and Scouters.

Decide how you'll prepare your food.

Some methods of cooking, such as gas stoves and grills, create less impact than others, such as open fires. Low-impact principles are followed when using a camp Dutch oven with charcoal on a fire pan, provided that the pan is placed on bare soil or rock, and the coal ash is disposed of in a discreet and fire-safe manner.

When using open fire to cook, follow local fire restrictions and use an established fire ring instead of creating a new one. Keep fires small. Collect wood from the ground rather than from standing trees. To avoid creating barren earth, find wood farther away from camp. Select smaller pieces of wood, and burn them completely to ash. Afterward, make sure the fire is completely out, then scatter the ashes. Learn how to use a fire pan or mound fire to prevent scorching the ground and blackening rocks. Don't bring firewood from home to camp if the wood might harbor insects or disease harmful to the flora in your camp area.

Carefully select and repackage your food to minimize trash.

Tiny pieces of trash easily become litter. Avoid bringing small, individually packaged candies and other such food items. Twist ties and bread clips are easily lost when dropped. Remove the wrappers and repackage such foods into ziplock bags before leaving home; or use knots, instead of ties and clips, to seal bread bags and the like.

Metal containers and their lids, crushed beverage cans, and broken glass can easily cut or puncture trash sacks. Wrap them carefully before placing them in thin-wall trash bags. Minimize the use of glass in camp. Scan the camp carefully when packing up to ensure that no litter is left behind.

Minimize leftovers and dispose of food waste properly.

Leftover foods make for messier trash and cleanup. If poured on open ground, they are unsightly and unsanitary. If buried, animals will dig them up. Leftovers encourage problem animals to come into camp if not properly managed. Carefully plan your meals to reduce leftovers. And if any remain, share with others or carefully repackage and set aside in a protected place to eat at a later meal.

Dispose of used wash and rinse water (also called gray water) in a manner appropriate for your camping area. Before disposal, remove or strain food chunks from the gray water and place these with the trash. If no dedicated gray water disposal area is available, scatter the water outside of camp in an area free of sensitive vegetation and at least 200 feet from streams and lakes. Avoid excessive sudsing by using only the amount of detergent necessary for the job. Bring only biodegradable soap to camp.

Plan to protect your food, trash, and other odorous items from animals.

Consider avoiding the use of very aromatic foods that can attract animals. Store food, trash, and other odorous items where animals won't be able to get to them. Besides being potentially dangerous to the animal, and inconvenient for the camper, trash is often spread over a large area once the animal gains access. Follow local regulations regarding proper food storage.

Decide whether to avoid collecting wild foods.

Don't harvest wild foods, such as berries, if these are not plentiful in the area you're visiting. Such scarce foods are likely to be a more important component of the local ecosystem.

These are only a few of the practical considerations and potential applications of the principles of the Scout Outdoor Code and Leave No Trace. Visit www.LNT.org for additional information and ideas.

Careless actions in camp can create problems for both humans and wildlife. PATRICIA SPYRAKOS/FLICKR.COM

Appendix E

RELATED RANK AND MERIT BADGE REQUIREMENTS

The following list summarizes all current Boy Scout merit badge requirements related to food preparation that can be accomplished by using the instructional material and recipes in *The Scout's Dutch Oven Cookbook*.

Keep in mind that rank and merit badge requirements are updated by BSA on a regular basis, and the identification numbers and details for these may change from those shown here. Regardless, the list will point you in the right direction and give a good picture of how this book can be used to satisfy the requirements specific to a given rank or badge.

Rank Advancement

Tenderfoot

3 Assist with preparing and cooking a meal for your patrol on a campout.

Second Class

2(g) Plan and cook one hot breakfast or lunch for yourself in camp over an open fire.

First Class

4(a) Help plan a patrol menu consisting of at least one breakfast, one lunch, and one dinner, two meals of which must be cooked.

4(b) Make a list showing the food amounts required to feed three or more boys and secure the ingredients.

4(c) Describe which pans, utensils, and other gear are required to cook and serve these meals.

4(d) Explain the procedures to follow in the safe handling and storage of perishable food products. Tell how to properly dispose of camp rubbish.

4(e) On a campout, serve as patrol cook and supervise an assistant in building the cooking fire. Prepare the meals from 4(a). Supervise cleanup.

Merit Badges

Camping (Required for Eagle rank)

2 Learn and explain the Leave No Trace principles and Scout Outdoor Code. Plan how to put these into practice on your next outing.

4(b) Assist a Scout patrol or Webelos unit with menu planning for a campout.

6(b) Discuss the importance of camp sanitation and why water treatment is essential.

7(a) Make a checklist of patrol gear required for your campout.

8(c) Prepare a camp menu and explain how it would be different from a menu for a backpacking or float trip. Select recipes and make a food list for your patrol, planning for two breakfasts, three lunches, and two suppers. Discuss how to protect your food against bad weather, animals, and contamination.

8(d) Cook at least two of the meals from 8(c) in camp. Both cannot be from the same meal category (i.e., breakfast, lunch, or dinner).

10 Discuss how working through the requirements for this merit badge has taught you about personal health and safety as well as public health.

Chemistry

4(a) Cook an onion until translucent, and cook another until caramelized (brown in color). Compare the tastes to that of a raw onion.

Cooking

1(a) Describe the injuries that can arise while cooking.

1(b) Describe how meat, eggs, dairy products, and fresh vegetables should be stored, transported, and properly prepared for cooking.

3(a) Plan a menu for two straight days of camping (six meals total, consisting of two breakfasts, two lunches, and two dinners). One dinner must include a soup, meat, fish, or poultry, along with two fresh vegetables and a dessert.

3(b) The menu in 3(a) must include a one-pot dinner, not prepared with canned goods.

3(c) Make a list for the menu from 3(a) showing the food amounts required to feed three or more boys.

3(d) List the utensils required to prepare and serve the meals in 3(a).

4(a) Using the menu from 3(a), prepare for yourself and two others the two dinners, one of either lunch, and one of either breakfast. Time the cooking so that each course will be ready to serve at the proper time. The meals may be prepared during separate camping trips.

4(c) For each meal in 4(a), use safe food-handling practices. Following each meal, dispose of all rubbish properly and clean the campsite thoroughly.

Fire Safety

10(b) Demonstrate setting up and putting out a cooking fire.

10(d) Explain how to set up a campsite safe from fire.

Fishing

9   Cook a fish that you have caught.

Fly Fishing

10   Cook a fish that you have caught.

Discuss with your Merit Badge Counselor how to best apply this book for the specific rank and merit badges you are working toward.

INDEX

About the Authors

Experienced campers, backpackers, and outdoor chefs, Tim and Christine Conners are the authors of *The Scout's Outdoor Cookbook, The Scout's Dutch Oven Cookbook, The Scout's Large Groups Cookbook,* and *The Scout's Backpacking Cookbook,* each a collection of unique and outstanding camp recipes from Scout leaders across the United States. Tim and Christine are also the authors of *Lipsmackin' Backpackin',* one of the most popular trail cookbooks of the past decade.

Tim and Christine have been testing outdoor recipes for over fifteen years now. At the invitation of Boy Scouts of America, the Conners have twice served as judges for *Scouting* magazine's prestigious national camp food cooking contest.

The Conners have four children, James, Michael, Maria, and David, their youngest. Tim is Assistant Scoutmaster and Christine is Committee Member and Merit Badge Counselor for the Coastal Empire Council's Troop 340 in Statesboro, Georgia, where their two oldest sons have attained the rank of Life Scout and are on the road to Eagle.

Outdoor Conners family activities include camping and day-hiking in the local state parks, backpacking on the Appalachian Trail, and kayaking on the region's lakes and rivers . . . when they aren't writing cookbooks.

Stop by www.scoutcooking.com to say howdy!

The Conners family shares dinner along the Appalachian Trail.
DAVID LATTNER